Introducing Social Work

Lena Dominelli

polity

First published in 2009 by Polity Press

Polity Press
65 Bridge Street
Cambridge CB2 1UR, UK

Polity Press
350 Main Street
Malden, MA 02148, USA

ISBN-13: 978-0-7456-4086-0
ISBN-13: 978-0-7456-4087-7(pb)

A catalogue record for this book is available from the British Library.

Typeset in 10 on 12 pt Sabon
by SNP Best-set Typesetter Ltd, Hong Kong
Printed and bound in Great Britain by MPG Books Ltd, Bodmin, Cornwall

For further information on Polity, visit our website: www.polity.co.uk

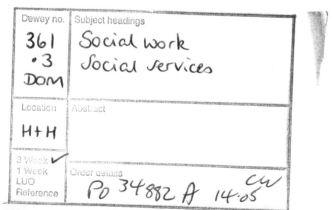

Introducing Social Work

To those creating a better world by working with others

Contents

Abbreviations

AA	Alcoholics Anonymous
ABSWAP	Association for Black Social Workers and Allied Professions
AMHP	Approved Mental Health Practitioner
ARS	Arrest Referral Scheme
ASBO	Anti-Social Behaviour Order
ASW	Approved Social Worker
BASW	British Association of Social Workers
BCODP	British Council of Organizations of Disabled People
CA	Corporate Assessment
CAF	Common Assessment Framework
CAFCASS	Children and Family Court Advisory Service
CAMHS	Children and Adolescent Mental Health Services
CARAT	Counselling, Assessment, Referral, Advice and Throughcare
CBT	cognitive-behavioural therapy
CCA	Community Care Act
CEHR	Commission on Equalities and Human Rights
CIL	Centre for Independent Living
CJB	Criminal Justice Board
CRB	Criminal Records Bureau
CRC	Convention on the Rights of the Child

CRE	Commission on Race Equality
CRPD	Convention on the Rights of Persons with Disabilities
CSCI	Commission for Social Care Inspection
CSWE	Council for Social Work Education
CWDC	Children's Workforce Development Council
DDA	Disability Discrimination Act
DETR	Department of Environment, Transport and the Regions
DfES	Department for Education and Skills
DH	Department of Health
DP	direct payment
DRC	Disability Rights Commission
DTO	Detention and Training Order
DTTO	Drug Treatment and Testing Order
EBP	evidence-based practice
EHR	European Human Rights (Act)
EOC	Equal Opportunities Commission
EPO	Emergency Protection Order
FAS	Foetal Alcohol Syndrome
FASD	Foetal Alcohol and Substance Disorder
FAST	Families and Survivors of the Tsunami
FEMA	Federal Emergency Management Agency
FGC	Family Group Conference
GATS	General Agreement on Trades and Services
GSCC	General Social Care Council
HC	Healthcare Commission
HMPS	Her Majesty's Prison Service
IASSW	International Association of Schools of Social Work
IB	individual budget
IBB	Independent Barring Board
IFSW	International Federation of Social Workers
IT	intermediate treatment
JAR	Joint Area Review
LAC	Local Area Committee
LAR	Local Area Review
MHA	Mental Health Act
MMSE	Mini-Mental State Examination
NAPO	National Association of Probation Officers
NAYPIC	National Association of Young People In Care
NCVO	National Council for Voluntary Organizations
NOMS	National Offender Management Service
NOS	National Occupational Standards

NSF	National Service Framework
NSPCC	National Society for the Prevention of Cruelty to Children
NTA	National Treatment Agency
NVQ	National Vocational Qualification
Ofsted	Office for Standards in Education
ONS	Office of National Statistics
PALS	Patient Advice and Liaison Services
PFI	Private Finance Initiative
PPP	Public–Private Partnership
QAA	Quality Assurance Agency
RIPL	Rebuilding People's Lives Network
RSU	Rough Sleepers Unit
RSW	Registered Social Worker
SCODA	Standing Conference on Drug Abuse
SCQF	Scottish Credit and Qualification Framework
SfC	Skills for Care
SHARC	Shelter's Housing Action in Rural Communities
STC	secure training centre
STU	secure training unit
TOPSS	Training Organization for the Personal Social Services
UPIAS	Union of Physically Impaired People Against Segregation
VBS	Vetting and Barring Scheme
VSA	Volatile Substance Abuse
WH	Workforce Hub
YJB	Youth Justice Board
YJS	Youth Justice System
YOI	Young Offenders' Institution
YOT	Youth Offending Team

Acknowledgements

Writing this book has been a real challenge. Social work is a profession I feel passionately about, but it is also a complex and difficult one to examine and convey to those not already committed to professional services in the care of others. For this book, I have consulted with a range of practitioners who are engaged in working on some of the most intractable social problems of our time. They deserve to be honoured for dealing seriously with people in damaging social circumstances, often held down by the weight of structural inequalities that thwart their life chances. I have felt privileged to have had these conversations with you. Although I take responsibility for the words I have written in these pages, I hope I have done justice to your endeavours and that you will recognize your work in its complexities in this endeavour. I thank you from the bottom of my heart for having made this writing possible.

I also thank my colleagues at Durham University and my family, especially Mom, David, Nicholas, Maria, Connie, Nic, Rita and Sam for their extensive encouragement and support when I would have rather given up. And to Emma Longstaff at Polity Press, thank you for giving me the opportunity to write something different.

Lena Dominelli

Introducing Social Work

Social work is an exciting profession. It is the only one charged with looking after people's general well-being in many different situations and various settings. It can be creative and adventurous while operating within a country's law and policies. Locality-based and specific in its remit, social work addresses issues that cross borders, tackling a particular blend of connections between the local and the global in concerns as diverse as: the sex trade in children; international adoptions; migrations linked to natural disasters and armed conflict; traffic in drugs; and organized crime. Ideally, social workers can support any person in need at any stage in the life cycle from birth to death. They can give reassurance during: difficult transitions in life; recuperation from accidents at home or the workplace; periods of grief; and recovery from natural disasters. Anyone can have need of a social worker. Those who do should be able to count on the one who responds being a skilled professional, able to work with them respectfully, efficiently and empathetically.

Social workers are expected to have an extensive range of knowledge, skills and appropriate values. How these are translated in specific contexts is disputed and provides the profession with considerable heterogeneity and porous borders. Social work's broad scope can confuse people about what social workers do and how they do it. In this book, I explore this profession and take readers through major activities and dilemmas that social workers encounter. I root my explorations within a social justice perspective but invite readers to examine this and form their own opinions of its value and worth. I see the profession's capacity to explore disagreements and controversies within its ranks as strengths that help it grow. In the limited space I have here, I can cover only a few items. I have chosen those I find indicative of the profession as a whole and illustrate transferable skills used in moving from solving problems in one area to another. Change is a constant feature of social work, so I engage primarily with its enduring elements, instead of limiting it to current requirements in British social work. This enables me to explore international examples, think differently and look for lessons of use in improving practice in the UK. Understanding the profession's generalities better equips people for practice in changing circumstances and engaging with transferable skills. I also highlight areas for future development in British social work training, e.g., disaster interventions.

With its remit to help any person in need, social work can lay claim to the right to become a universal, unstigmatized service available to all at the point of need. Realizing this ambition requires political will and society's commitment to releasing the necessary resources. In the UK, politicians have refused to unlock those required, despite calls to do so ever since 1942, when William Beveridge drew up his report outlining the foundations of the modern British welfare system. Only health and education were funded as universal services, and, by 2008, charges for some of these undermined their universality. Housing and the personal social services received minimal funding and became residual services targeting the neediest of needy people, i.e., those incapable of helping themselves. This is not the only way of delivering social services, and it raises the question of reviewing social work's role and mandate in society.

Social workers often find themselves in the headlines. This can be for positive reasons, like when they help people recover from calamities, as in the case of people who survived the fire at King's Cross station in 1987; railway disasters like that at Ladbroke Grove in 1999; the tsunami that burst on the shores of 12 countries bordering the Indian Ocean in 2004 (see chapter 9); and bombings in New York in 2001, Madrid in 2004 and London in 2005; or, less dramatically, when people need assistance in daily routines, as occurs when providing respite care to parents looking after disabled adult children. At other times, it is for negative reasons, when things go wrong, for example when children are murdered by their carers, as occurred to Victoria Climbié in February 2000. Social workers' difficulty in maintaining public confidence under stressful conditions and disputes about what constitutes good practice make social work a troubled and troubling profession. Nevertheless, when it supports people in practical ways, it is a much appreciated one. I explore these contradictions in these pages. How I do this reflects my particular approach to the profession, which has been one of researching its reaches, reflecting upon and questioning its dominant taken-for-granted assumptions and challenging educators and practitioners, including myself, to strive always to enhance our understanding and improve our practice. Thus, I refer to the profession's historical development, its global spread and local practices to provide easily understood insights into the complexities of what social workers do.

Structure of the Book

The profession's responses to practice have been contentious and bounded by its three key approaches: maintenance, therapeutic and emancipatory (Davies, 1985; Dominelli, 1997; Payne, 2005). These are contested by its adherents and professionals in other disciplines, especially psychiatry and psychology, who encroach upon its spheres of influence. This book is intended to introduce social work – the concept; its values and ethics; the work that social workers do; the expectations that others have about their work; and contradictions and dilemmas that they are required to resolve. Issues of oppression, including those affecting 'race', gender, class, age, disability and sexual orientation, are explored throughout the book because oppression can be encountered in any form of practice. Social workers are committed to avoiding oppression in their own work and finding ways of alleviating it in society. The key national context from which this book is written is the UK, but devolution has altered aspects of the profession in each of the four countries that constitute it. European harmonization, globalization and mass movements of peoples have altered the nature of social work in this nation-state. I take these into account by making connections between the locality-specific and broader concerns of the profession.

In chapter 1, I explore the different definitions of social work and controversies involved in what social work stands for. The remainder of the book focuses on social work interventions. In chapter 2, I examine working with children and families. This comprises one of the most difficult areas of practice, not least because social workers evaluate how parents and other carers raise children and, if their parenting is found wanting, have the power to remove those children from them. I use case studies involving older people to highlight dilemmas that social workers encounter in working with adults in chapter 3. Chapter 4 is concerned with social work with disabled people. They have challenged social workers' failure to address the social dimensions of disability, especially society's disabling nature and reliance on the medical model of disability, because this disempowers disabled people.

In chapter 5, I examine social workers' interventions in a specific area of expertise: mental ill health. Additional qualifications have been required of social workers who have provided services to people with mental health problems, because they work in an extremely difficult area with other professionals, like psychiatrists, and are involved in 'sectioning' people or admitting them to psychiatric hospitals for treatment with or without their permission. I consider the plight of homeless people, particularly young homeless people who live on the streets, in chapter 6. Using their own stories, I highlight how they survive by networking with each other to survive hardship. In chapter 7, I highlight the difficulties encountered in working with people who abuse drugs and alcohol. These difficulties arise because substance misusers also experience several other problems, such as homelessness, unemployment, poor schooling, social isolation and low self-esteem.

In chapter 8, I explore offending behaviour and the work of probation officers and social work professionals who work with offenders. Probation officers have a duty to protect society and help offenders mend their ways, a challenging and difficult task because offenders themselves have to ensure that their behaviours do not harm others. Government policies and legislation have a major impact on probation officers' work. They have also had a bad press, as in cases of high-profile sex offenders sexually abusing children while out 'on licence' (release before a prison sentence is completed), or mentally disordered offenders who kill people when placed in the community with controls that fail to ensure that medication is taken as required.

Disasters provide another setting in which social workers intervene to support people. Disasters can be human-made, as occurred in Bhopal, India, in 1984, when equipment failure at a Union Carbide plant led to massive pollution of the atmosphere and killed and injured thousands of people. Or they can be natural disasters, as occurred during: volcanic eruptions in Monserrat since 1995; the earthquake in Bam, Iran, in 2003; Hurricanes Ivor and Wilma in the Caribbean in 2004; the Indian Ocean tsunami of 2004; Hurricane Katrina in the USA in 2005; or the floods in Britain in 2007. Some natural disasters are recurrent: for example, the Caribbean had barely recovered from previous hurricanes when others of devastating force struck, as did Hurricane Dean in 2007. Moreover, the number of these devastating hurricanes is set to increase, with global warming predicted to cause more of those rated Category 5. Social workers intervene in the immediate aftermath of major catastrophes by: providing short-term relief by means of food, shelter and medicine; helping those affected to deal with the psychological traumas that these events cause; and becoming involved in long-term reconstruction endeavours. I explore this facet of social work in chapter 9.

The personal social services help people: deal with transitions in their lives; overcome hardships; improve their functioning in difficult circumstances; and assume greater control of their lives. I conclude with a plea for making high-quality publicly funded social work services available to all. This requires social services to become universal provisions that are rooted in the welfare state and part of a social contract between individuals and the state. If created on this basis, these will affirm citizenship in a just society, or what T.H. Marshall (1970) called 'social citizenship'. Social citizenship is based on solidarity, mutuality and reciprocity between citizens. The pooling of social resources through taxation makes it possible to have these services available free to all at the point of need. Social workers who pursue this objective would locate their practice within the emancipatory school of practice. This can be seen as a political act, which invites its own controversies.

1

What is Social Work?

There is a knock on the door. Gladys, an elderly woman immobilized by arthritis, opens it, leaving the chain in place, to see a young, fresh-faced woman on her doorstep. 'Who are you?' she asks suspiciously.

'Your social worker,' she replies.

'I don't need any help,' Gladys answers and begins to shut the door.

Social workers' sphere of action is 'the social', or the site where people interact with each other and their environment. Social workers engage in it by intervening in social problems experienced by individuals, groups or communities and aim to help people regain control of their situations. Their work can cover any aspect of people's lives from cradle to grave. Arranging personal social services for service users (clients) is a major task that social workers perform. They can encounter ethical dilemmas when delivering services, even when claimants are eligible for them. Some of these arise in reconciling limited resources with identified needs, especially if budgets do not cover these. Social workers take account of service user reactions to their interventions when deciding whether to provide resources.

Social workers can encounter hostility and suspicion because people fear their powers to control their behaviour through legislative authority and access to resources. Another form of control is social workers' power to deprive people of their liberty by being placed in residential facilities when they wish to remain in their own homes. Their exercise of such powers is restricted by legislation and professional codes of ethics to prevent abuse. While social workers' interventions in child protection may often be resented, their contributions to people's well-being in practical ways is much appreciated.

In this chapter, I explore different definitions of and expectations about social work and identify key features. Notions of social justice and human rights are central to contemporary social work and underpin its basic values. These are usually demonstrated in concrete practical ways rather than as abstract concepts. I consider these issues by asking:

- What is the domain of 'the social' or the various settings in which social workers intervene?
- Who does social work?
- Who employs social workers?
- What are social workers' responsibilities to service users, their employers and society, locally, nationally and internationally?

I use case materials to focus on social work as a dynamic system that reflects and adapts to the changing nature of society and occasionally influences its direction.

Defining Social Work

Social work is a caring profession undertaken in the social sphere. What constitutes the 'social' is a matter of controversy, but it is generally assumed to be an interactive space that involves people in relationships of commitment to each other's well-being, often sanctioned by the state. Social work is variously defined. At its simplest, it is about helping others and occurs as both formal and informal helping in response to those needing assistance. Definitions of social work distinguish between formal and informal care to mark out the terrain of professional practice. Informal aid is associated with kind displays of caring and affection proffered by people one knows as an act of love or unpaid altruism when enacted by strangers, compared to professional assistance or formal help given by qualified paid workers.

Informal Helping or Systematically Improving Well-Being

Formal helping involves systematic attempts to improve well-being and functioning. It is attached to organizations or institutions specifically designed for the purpose, has paid professionals in charge of its activities and exists in public, voluntary and commercial settings. Formal care has been subjected to professionalization processes that aim to lay down a scientific basis to and professional controls over helping endeavours. Social work's informal elements can be found everywhere as assistance offered by family, friends, neighbours and volunteers. The presence of informal care carries implications for formal care. At times, informal care complements formal care, e.g., when family and friends contribute to formal packages of care devised for older people. At other times, informal care precludes the need for formal care, as happens when a family cares for a disabled adult without state intervention. Both are usually carried out by women and assumed to draw on women's 'natural' capacities to help others. There are overlaps in skills between formal and informal care. This ideological stance identifies a small part of social work's remit and ignores its professional expertise. Virginia Bottomley, Secretary of State for Health in Thatcherite Britain, thought that 'any streetwise granny' could do social work. In the popular imagination social work is associated with caring skills held by mature persons.

Formal social work, also known as *professional social work*, differentiates itself from informal care. Professional social work involves broader responsibilities and accountabilities than help given by friends, neighbours or relatives. *Professional* social work engages in a more sophisticated understanding of people's behaviour and reasons for acting as they do and employs a more systematic rationale for intervening in people's lives in particular ways. Professional social workers also seek to explain why certain behaviours are acceptable and others are not from society's point of view. Its practitioners attempt to balance individual self-interest with social responsibility and work within legislative and policy remits. Professional social workers require training to fulfil more complicated sets of responsibilities and intervene effectively. Unless indicated otherwise, I use the term 'social work' to refer to professional social work. Social workers' expertise is considerable. They deal with some of the most socially excluded people in society, those with extremely complicated social problems and those whom other professionals have decided cannot benefit from their interventions.

Social work's *professional* mandate covers a lot of ground, has indeterminate borders and requires a considerable number of skills, including those of making connections between people and life circumstances that may be far from obvious. As formal care, social work exists in many countries across the globe, each with its own variants of how it should be done, what it should do and who should do it. People can talk about social work, community work, social development work, group work, individual work, therapeutic work, and still remain within the boundaries of the profession (Dominelli, 2006). An idea of its heterogeneity is given by its two key international organizations. The International Federation of Social Workers (IFSW) claims that there are over 1.5 million social workers located in 84 countries, over 470,000 of whom are its members. The International Association of Schools of Social Work (IASSW) has identified 3000 schools of social work offering professional qualifications at tertiary level in 74 countries. This diversity makes a comprehensive definition of social work difficult.

Definitions of professional social work are varied. Eileen Younghusband (1964: 39) suggests that social work centres on 'social problems arising from the interrelation between man [sic] and his [sic] social environment'. Katherine Kendall (1978: 43) continues this refrain, stating that social work's professionalism relies on a capacity to

> assess the nature of the need and the problem, to estimate the capacity of the person to handle the problem, to foster every inner strength of the person toward the goal of finding his [sic] own solution, and to utilise all the outer resources of the environment and the community which might be of value in this problem-solving endeavour.

These definitions capture social work's key dimensions, but have been critiqued for focusing too much on the personal inadequacies of individuals and not enough on the structural causes of problems (Bailey and Brake, 1975; Dominelli, 1997). In contemporary Britain, a further debate has opened up between social work and social care, without clearly distinguishing between them (Higham, 2005). Government policy emphasizes social care, which is associated with the physical care of people, as occurs in many community care initiatives. Academic discourses favour social work as the broader professional remit, with social care as a subset within this wider classification. In it, social care is a specialist service that requires a set of competences in financial management, the purchasing or commissioning of services and relating to people.

The international definition of social work accepted by the membership of the IASSW and IFSW in 2000 and jointly declared as such by both organizations in 2001 attempts to transcend the problems of defining the role and purpose of social work by focusing on changing individual and societal elements. The former addresses problematic interpersonal behaviour, the latter structural inequalities. According to the definition:

> The social work profession promotes social change, problem solving in human relationships and the empowerment and liberation of people to enhance well-being. Utilising theories of human behaviour and social systems, social work intervenes at the points where people interact with their environments. Principles of human rights and social justice are fundamental to social work. (IASSW–IFSW, 2004)

This broad definition of social work suggests that many different kinds of expertise, ranging from advocacy to forensic social work and counselling, are subsumed by the 'social worker' title.

Some countries regulate the profession more than others. Regulatory arrangements seek to protect vulnerable people from charlatans who might exploit service user vulnerability by holding social workers accountable and requiring them to adhere to codes of practice consistent with the aim of minimizing harm. Registration is a system of controlling professional behaviour and maintaining standards in practice. Since 2003, the title 'social worker' in the UK has been protected or restricted to those registered with a regulatory body, the General Social Care Council (GSCC). The GSCC can remove practitioners found guilty of violating professional norms from the list of approved title holders and bar them from future practice. To practise in England, social workers now register with the GSCC to acquire the title 'Registered Social Worker' (RSW). In some parts of the USA, social workers have to be both registered and licensed. In the UK, registration has not encompassed all those who do social work within its remit. For example, personal advisers, Sure Start workers, care managers and those who work with young offenders do social work but are not called social workers and are not required to register as such.

Multiple Roles, Accountabilities and Responsibilities

Social workers have many responsibilities. Key amongst these is enhancing people's well-being. In undertaking this task, they act as:

- *facilitators* who enable others to reach their objectives;
- *gatekeepers* who (dis)allow access to social resources and services;

- *regulators* who control unacceptable behaviours to maintain social order and minimize service users' capacities to harm themselves or others;
- *upholders* of people's human rights and citizenship status; and
- advocates for change.

At times, these roles place social workers in contradictory positions or those that are oppositional to each other. Tensions between caring for people and controlling them can place social workers in what are called *care–control dilemmas*. Resolving these is complicated when different principles conflict, as occurs when social workers balance self-determination with reducing harm. Social workers are expected to work with these contradictions without making mistakes because people's lives or livelihoods are at stake. This expectation is impossible to meet all the time because, being human, social workers make mistakes. As person-centred, proficient, reflective practitioners, social workers strive for excellence in all they do. Their record of meeting this objective is more than respectable, but the media cover mainly instances in which social workers 'fail' service users (even if social workers are not responsible for the failure). Thus, their many successful interventions are unseen by the public eye.

Like Janus in Roman mythology, social workers face both ways at once – helping people and controlling them simultaneously. They are criticized for doing too much and doing too little. In the Cleveland Child Abuse Scandal of the 1980s, social workers were accused of being over-zealous and inventing child sexual abuse where there was none (Bell, 1985; Butler-Sloss, 1988). Ten years after the initial outcry against practitioners, this stance was exposed as having failed children (Campbell, 1997). And, as the courts had returned children to their abusers for care, their interests as children in need of protection were not secured. In other cases, where children are physically abused until they die, social workers have been accused of not doing enough, as occurred when Victoria Climbié was murdered by her great-aunt, Marie-Thérèse Kouao, and Marie-Thérèse's boyfriend (Laming, 2003). *The balance that social workers have to find is the fine line between care and control that enables them to empower people in making their own decisions while at the same time ensuring that they do not fall foul of the law, contravene socially accepted norms or harm themselves or others.* Social workers are often caught in controversies about what they should do and what they actually do.

Different Social Work Approaches to Interventions

Social workers' responses to requests for services are embedded in the three types of professional intervention noted in the introduction: maintenance, therapeutic and emancipatory (Dominelli, 1997; Payne, 2005). Each has a specific focus and approach to problems, despite overlaps between them, especially in meeting individual needs. Beyond that, each is committed to different ways of linking the personal to the social or ignoring it.

The *maintenance* school reflects a conventional view of social work. It aims to improve individual functioning or adaptation to situations and emphasizes neutral professionals who objectively examine a person's circumstances. Assistance is provided on the basis of clearly defined, often bureaucratic, criteria. An example is assessing an older person's need for aid and adaptations strictly in terms of current physical health and eligibility for services. There is no attempt to ascertain whether lack of provisions now might cause deterioration later that would require even more public resources like health care. Nor does it ask a practitioner to consider the impact of policies on resource availability for certain needs or the appropriateness of eligibility criteria for groups of people who might be routinely excluded. Maintenance social workers are more likely to focus simply on individual (and family relationships) without noticing that many individuals with similar problems expose larger social issues. This is illustrated by a maintenance social worker who helps an older person claim all benefit entitlements to raise income levels. This intervention matters: 40 per cent of older people do not claim benefits, thus losing £4.5 billion a year (Sefton, 2007). But in following the maintenance approach, this worker would not be concerned about inadequate benefit levels, or seek to change these, or respond to not claiming as a problem affecting many.

The *therapeutic* approach is an off-shoot of the maintenance school, but focuses primarily on what an individual can do to improve his or her position through targeted professional interventions. A principal aim is to enhance psychological and emotional functioning so that a person can handle his or her own affairs. This is instanced by an older woman who cannot form friendships with strangers because she fears they might attack her. She has caught burglars in her home and been seriously beaten up. This experience left her suspicious of people she does not know and disinclined to interact with them as a form of self-protection. A therapeutic approach to her situation offers her trauma counselling to help re-establish her equilibrium and learn how to relate to other people as possible friends rather than merely as foes. Addressing the causes of criminal behaviour would be left for other professionals.

The third school of social work, the *emancipatory* approach, is associated with radical social work and questions the current balance of power in society and distribution of resources. It identifies the oppressive nature of contemporary social relations and argues that social workers have a responsibility to do something about these while helping people as individuals by, for example, addressing racial oppression in and through social work practice. This is exemplified by a law centre worker who offers a low-income family of Asian descent advice on how to sponsor older parents as immigrants to the UK and focuses both on giving advice *and* changing the law. Immigration rules require those sponsoring relatives to guarantee that they will not be a 'burden on the state' by requiring welfare state resources (Cohen, 2001). The family is worried that it will be difficult to adhere to this requirement for more than a few years because they and their children are ageing and will need more financial resources for themselves. Besides advising them, the law centre worker decides to form a group to lobby parliament to change a law that penalizes poor families more than wealthy ones because the additional financial burdens on poor people's resources may outstrip their capacity to provide in the longer term. This worker is engaging in emancipatory social work that combines advocacy on changing policy with individual work.

The emancipatory approach is concerned with ensuring social justice at the individual, group and community levels and seeking structural changes to make this happen. Its practitioners help people organize to change their communities and/or government policies. If mobilizing communities, they are called community workers. Though they constitute part of the social work profession, community activists in the UK are less favoured now than they were in the 1970s. The activist community dimension of social work is disputed in the maintenance school claim that emancipatory social work involves social workers in political activity best left to politicians (Davies, 1985).

Each of these approaches is legitimate, but the one that is adopted reflects the values a social worker draws upon to resolve ethical dilemmas and decide what to do in a given situation. Each has similarities with the others alongside differences. For example, the aims of helping an individual, group or community to enhance capacity, take responsibility for particular behaviours and make decisions that improve coping skills are held in common. So are some skills, e.g., interviewing people and making needs assessments in specific cases. Key differences focus on attitudes to change and wider society. These include questions about the appropriateness of supporting group mobilizations or influencing changes in society while helping individuals. Only the emancipatory school accepts the legitimacy of all three activities, seeing the removal of structural inequalities as essential to ensuring social justice at the individual level. Feminist social workers, for example, illustrate this in practice by paying particular attention to the links between the personal predicament of individual women and their position in the wider social structures. This stance is indicated in the slogans 'the personal is political' and 'the political is personal' and evident in this book.

This variety makes defining what a social worker does a complicated and messy business. As indicated above, social workers can be found in a vast array of settings, performing a wide range of interventions. Younghusband (1978) has divided these into: casework or work with individuals; group work; and community work. The boundaries between these are blurred. Nowadays, social workers may be undertaking individual or one-to-one work with a particular person whilst insisting that they participate in some kind of group activity or even community endeavour. This approach is used regularly in work with offenders or persons misusing substances, because they are required to undertake work in groups to address issues related to their own individual behaviour: for example, attending a therapeutic group alongside the requirement to work with and report regularly to a named professional like a counsellor or probation officer in a given location at a specified time for individual sessions. Combination orders (those that combine probation orders with community service orders) given to offenders involve individual therapeutic and group activities.

A Profession with Multiple Accountabilities and a Professional Identity

Social work is a contextualized discipline, i.e., it takes place in specific contexts. It is dominated by the boundaries of the nation-state, but often transcends them to cater for: internationalized social problems like international adoptions and the sex trade in children; the impact of globalization and market imperatives; a wide range of employing agencies; and national and international legislation and social policies. In the UK, 105 local authorities and 25,000 private and voluntary agencies employ people who do social work (Horner, 2007). The number of private and independent sector providers of social services is likely to increase as the General Agreement on Trades and Services (GATS) becomes implemented. GATS is an international treaty aiming to increase the role of the market in health, education and social services and foster further change by integrating the profession more fully into the marketplace. Learning from other countries is useful in responding to these changes.

Social work is a profession with multiple accountabilities – to employers; service users/clients; policymakers; professionals in associated disciplines like medicine, psychiatry, psychology and law; and the public. It is a constantly changing profession whose role and purpose in society is often disputed and subjected to professional and governmental regulation. Its constantly fragmenting boundaries and changing nature enable social work activities to be appropriated by other professionals: for example, the completion of risk assessments in child abuse cases by child psychologists; and the opening up of mental health work formerly undertaken by Approved Social Workers to any professional without a social work degree. Similar shifts are happening in elder care as it becomes embedded in community care and care management. Social work is constantly being restructured by the state and emerging in different forms while retaining its core tasks of caring for people and regulating behaviour.

The profession has struggled to secure its scientific basis, credibility and professional status since its inception, not least because it wanted to define a profession differently from that prevailing in medicine by focusing on *social* relationships rather than the symptoms of problems, and it was staffed primarily by women, whose work was and still is socially devalued (Walton, 1975; Dominelli, 2002b). Social work's capacity to borrow concepts and theories from other disciplines and adapt these for its own purposes is seen as a sign of immaturity not one of interdependence between subject areas.

Social Work Competences, Values, Skills and Education

Social workers are required to adhere to specific professional values, to have the skills and competencies to intervene effectively and to be able to transfer knowledge from area to area. Knowledge is acquired and tested by training that provides a pathway to registration. Degree-level professional qualifications began in Britain in 2003 with generic studies. Specialist expertise and training is pursued afterwards, mainly with post-qualifying and advanced awards. This might change in favour of more specialist training as the division into children's services and adult services is consolidated. Scotland has already introduced a benchmark for a Scottish Credit and Qualification Framework (SCQF) Level 9 Award as the Standard for Childhood Practice. From 2008, all those working as lead practitioners and managers in children's services have to obtain this 360-credit qualification. From 2011, those currently qualified and registered with the Scottish Social Services Council must gain this award before re-registration.

Social work competences in England are specified and monitored by the GSCC using key roles and National Occupational Standards (NOS) (DH, 2002b). Similar bodies oversee social work in the other three nations – Scotland, Wales and Northern Ireland; the Scottish Social Services Council, the Care Council for Wales and the Northern Ireland Social Care Council, respectively. The six key roles defined by the Training Organization for the Personal Social Services (TOPSS) and considered transferable (TOPSS, 2002) are:

- prepare for and work with individuals, families, carers, groups and communities to assess their needs and circumstances;
- plan, carry out, review and evaluate social work practice with individuals, families, carers, groups, communities and other professionals;
- support individuals to represent their needs, views and circumstances;
- manage risk to individuals, families, carers, groups, communities, self and colleagues;
- manage and be accountable, with supervision and support, for your own social work practice within your organization;
- demonstrate professional competence in social work practice.

Some universities, e.g., Southampton, have added demonstrating anti-oppressive practice competencies as a seventh key role. Others incorporate these as values elements. TOPSS was replaced by the Children's Workforce Development Council (CWDC) for children's services and Skills for Care (SfC) for adult services in 2005. These organizations have retained the focus on key roles and NOS as the basis for social work education, but are layered with further learning requirements. The Department of Health (DH, 2002b) has identified the required areas of learning and assessment as:

- assessment, planning, intervention and review;
- communication skills;
- partnership working across professional disciplines and agencies;
- law;
- human growth and development.

The Quality Assurance Agency (QAA) also formulated subject benchmark statements for incorporation in courses. Social work's benchmark statement was reviewed in 2007. It currently requires students to 'acquire, critically evaluate, apply and integrate knowledge and understanding' in five core areas of study. These are:

- social work services and service users;
- the context of service delivery;
- values and ethics;
- social work theory;
- social work practice.

The *processes* of social work focus on how things are done and how practitioners involve those accessing services. Key ones in practice are: assessment; planning; implementation or intervention; and evaluation. Each of these is an ongoing process that feeds into and out of the others. This makes social work processes complex and often circular rather than a set of neat linear steps, though theorists like Compton and Galaway (2006) have nevertheless tried to fit these within a linear framework. They define the processes of intervention as having a beginning, middle and end that follow sequentially. Whilst conducting these processes, social workers communicate, engage, plan, assess and evaluate for and/or with others. A requirement to undertake research is absent.

Social work interventions have to occur within legislative parameters, an ethical framework and code of professional ethics to ensure that social workers do not take advantage of people in vulnerable positions, especially if they are mentally ill, infirm or too young to speak up for what they want. Ethics are regulatory codes that guide professional behaviour and reduce power differentials between individuals requiring services and those providing them. These regulate behaviour to reduce the likelihood of professionals abusing service users. Ethical codes are based on the principles or values that a profession adopts. Codes of ethics are often defined within a national context through a professional association. In England, the British Association of Social Workers (BASW) has enshrined these in its *Code of Ethics*. It endorses the values of social justice, empowerment and non-judgementality. The GSCC has also devised a *Code of Practice* for practitioners and employers. The IASSW and IFSW have agreed an ethical document and global standards for qualifying practice that transcend narrow national boundaries. These go alongside the international definition that prioritizes social change and social justice as fundamental principles in social work. These documents can be downloaded from their respective websites.

The traditional values that underpin social work's code of ethics were initially voiced by Father Biestek (1961), a Jesuit priest who articulated these around the Kantian moral principle of 'respect for' or 'dignity of' the person (Banks, 2006). Their meaning has changed a little over time, mainly in the wording, but their expression as values remains relevant today. Biestek stipulated social work's values as:

- *individualization* – a focus on the uniqueness of each individual's situation;
- *purposeful expression of feelings* – using emotion to initiate behavioural change;
- *controlled emotional involvement* – maintaining a professional distance in relationships with service users;
- *acceptance* – valuing a person in his or her own right;
- *non-judgemental attitude* – refraining from passing judgement on others as people (while condemning unacceptable behaviour);
- *self-determination* – promoting service user independence and ability to make decisions about their lives;
- *confidentiality* – not disclosing information obtained in a professional relationship.

These values have encouraged social workers to work with individuals in respectful, non-judgemental ways that empower them to control their own lives. For instance, social workers who help children address grief and loss when parents separate, divorce or become terminally ill display these values. The words and contexts may have altered over time; the values and meanings have not. Key changes to Biestek's values have been: using contingent confidentiality to make explicit the limits to confidentiality; adopting empowerment to signal going beyond self-determination; embracing social justice and social change as legitimate aims of practice; addressing the failure of current arrangements to promote people's well-being; and transferring these values to new subjects. Contingent confidentiality is the term used to define the boundaries within which confidentially can be maintained. This explanation of the limits to confidentiality should occur at the beginning of a professional relationship to enable the practitioner to avoid getting into a contradictory situation of promising complete confidentiality and then being unable to deliver because the service user discloses something illegal which they are obliged to report to the relevant authorities, e.g., sexually abusing a child (Dominelli, 2002c).

Service users should not be abused by practitioners in any profession. Abuse by social workers, whilst rare, does occur. As it does, we have to ask why. We also have to consider what constitutes abuse, as it ranges from name-calling to physical and sexual assaults or murder. I define as abuse any attempt to remove or lessen individuals' capacity to think or act for themselves if the intent is to humiliate or belittle. Abuse is morally corrupt and unacceptable behaviour that can be perpetuated by individuals, groups or institutions. In Sweden, the power of words to damage confidence is recognized by law to prevent adults from using abusive language that can undermine a child's self-esteem, e.g., calling a child 'stupid' instead of referring to behaviour as silly or inappropriate. Social workers who, owing to lack of time or resources, refuse to visit older people who reject help are behaving unethically as this can lead to neglect.

Abuse becomes institutionalized when it is embedded in policies and routine practices that give precedence to bureaucratic norms rather than individual needs for care, as it was in Pindown, a high-profile abuse case involving social care workers. Those workers who thought the Pindown regime in Staffordshire was abusive were reluctant to challenge the manager's definition of appropriate practice with children, enabling the abuse to continue for years (Levy and Kahan, 1991). The institutionalization of abuse makes it harder to challenge. Despite precautions and mechanisms to regulate social workers' behaviour, some have abused service users in the guise of protecting them. This has occurred in aversion therapies used as behaviour modification techniques to control children with disruptive behaviour, including those now diagnosed as autistic. Fear of reprisals is one key to the failure of workers and children to report abusers. Lack of adequate training for residential care staff is another (Warner, 1992). 'Whistleblowing' procedures were created to empower workers to tackle such abuse by divulging their concerns and protecting their job security when doing so. Moreover, abuse by professionals can be punished via professional procedures and criminal or civil courts. Sarah Banks (2002) has researched the GSCC's de-registration of social workers accused of professional misconduct to examine this issue in greater depth (see also GSCC, 2008).

Children, disabled people and those experiencing mental ill health are not the only user groups to be abused. Elder abuse also occurs and can devastate individual lives. Carers have been charged with abusing older people in private homes. For example, at the Maypole Nursing Home in Birmingham, 28 people died in 2002 (CSCI, 2003). Closing homes when older people do not wish to leave can constitute institutional abuse, because individuals have no say in what happens as the power to make decisions resides with owners and managers. Massive home closures in Birmingham in 2001 precipitated a care crisis for older people. Service users and professionals protested against these as violations of human rights (BBC News, 2001).

Techno-Bureaucratic Social Work Replaces Relational Social Work

How social workers do their jobs has constantly shifted. At its inception as a profession over 100 years ago in Europe (Kendall, 2000), relationship-building was central to helping people improve their position. Relationship-building, key to social workers' capacity to act as change agents, was encapsulated as relational social work (Folgheraiter, 2004). Relational social work initiates change in individual behaviour by establishing a trusted and trusting relationship between workers and service users. Time is given to listen actively to those being helped and engaging them in defining a plan of action to best meet their specific needs. Overworked statutory workers in the UK have little time for relationship-building, with the result that relational social work has now been replaced by techno-bureaucratic social work. Statutory social workers view bureaucratic mechanisms as integral aspects of 'new' managerialist or public sector management regimes where managers regulate professional behaviour through bureaucratic means. In these, formulaic responses to need supersede the professional considerations that some managers claim impede service delivery.

Under care management and the 'new' managerialism that now governs social work, performance indicators limit the time spent on a case, and information technologies guide social workers in what options are available. This leaves practitioners with less space for professional judgements. Instead, responses are tailored to service users by bureaucratized or procedurally driven criteria that emphasize: packages of care to be delivered; how much each will cost; and who will deliver it, where and when. This approach highlights a bureau-technocratic slant to the profession that may overlook individual uniqueness. It can disillusion workers and service users with the facilities ultimately provided. Social workers have questioned this model's appropriateness. A social worker in a study in southern England claimed that in bureaucratic regimes:

> Work is increasingly becoming less related to needs and more towards resources or budgets. Due to increased workload [I have] much less time to spend using counselling type skills.

One suggested that 'choice is offered and then taken away'. Another said: 'We are so busy managing resources we are in danger of ignoring the people who need them' (Dominelli, 2004b: 168). This research also revealed a gulf between managers, who thought the system worked as intended, and social workers, who did not.

Relational social work has become the prerogative of the voluntary sector. Many statutory workers whose workloads have increased with extremely complicated cases have transferred to voluntary agencies where they can 'still do *real* social work'. Service users have challenged the bureau-technocratic approach and created their own services in the voluntary sector while increasingly making demands on mainstream statutory services. Their critiques, especially those voiced by women, black activists and disabled people, labelled social work an oppressive profession and challenged it to empower people and elevate expertise held by individuals alongside professional knowledge. They succeeded in doing this by initiating new forms of social work practice that are in keeping with emancipatory approaches, e.g., feminist social work, anti-racist social work, Afri-centric social work, social work from a black perspective and the social model of disability and mental health (John-Baptiste, 2001; Graham 2002; Dominelli, 2002a).

Social workers have responded to these challenges by developing empowering forms of practices based on the services their critics have developed. These include feminist social work and anti-racist social work. Social workers engage with agendas set by multiple stakeholders interested in the profession: employers, politicians, other professionals and the public. These are often contradictory, and stakeholders can easily scapegoat social workers, who are reluctant to defend their profession in the media or reveal details about specific cases. Practitioners' desire to be 100 per cent accurate also makes it difficult to argue that they did their best when things go wrong – a case that professionals like doctors and psychiatrists have less difficulty making. When Harold Shipman, GP, murdered 250 patients between 1971 and 1998 before getting caught, the medical profession was not brought into disrepute. Dame Janet Smith's report on the Shipman inquiry exposed systemic failings in holding medics accountable across their careers without pillorying doctors in general. In sharp contrast, social workers' entire profession is castigated when not they, but other carers, e.g., a mother's boyfriend, murder a child. For them, demands for wholesale changes to practice become unstoppable after an inquiry reports.

Reasons for differentiated responses to professional misconduct include: the low status accorded to social work as a female-dominated profession, which is the product of patriarchal gender relations that value work done by men but not women; and the fact that the medical profession itself defines what constitutes professional standards and remains above critique even when its practitioners do wrong. Social workers, embodying caring tasks that anyone can do, are easily labelled inadequate individuals who should not undertake activities they cannot handle (Batty, 2004). Social work practitioners and educators are attacked for defending oppressed people's demands for social justice when seen as acting outside their professional remit. The media hysteria around anti-racist social work in the summer of 1993 remains a classic instance of this. Journalists fabricated an intervention to discredit anti-racist practice and place social work educators and practitioners on trial for working for racial justice by labelling them 'politically correct' and incompetent (see Dunant, 1994).

Demands on practitioners are contradictory. Accounts of their predicament highlight contradictions between expectations and assessments of risk in given situations and the lack of resources that impede social workers in routine tasks. In these conditions, social workers have to: procure the resources they need to conduct their work; assess their capacity to weigh up risks; and respect an individual's right to refuse help. Social workers seem to be held accountable for what they do but also for what others do.

Case study: Working with families in Family Group Conferences

Harold is a 12-year-old white English boy caught on CCTV vandalizing a bus shelter. It is his first offence, but he is deemed 'beyond control' by his mother, Cynthia, who abuses drugs. His father is unknown. His social worker refers him for a Family Group

Conference (FGC), where all members of his extended family can work out a plan to keep him out of trouble. An FGC is a means of empowering families in making decisions about members. The FGC Coordinator facilitates the meeting and its decision-making processes. In Part 1, professionals share information with the family, including the resources available. In Part 2, the family is left alone, with the Coordinator nearby to answer questions and further facilitate discussions between family members. This FGC is lengthy, and various tensions surface between family members. Harold's mother's wishes are not taken seriously because she is a drug-user. Her father refuses to consider taking Harold because he is 'a constant liar and trouble-maker'. Her brother has children of his own and worries Harold will be a 'bad influence'. After much to-ing and fro-ing with the Coordinator encouraging the family to explore their differences and Harold's needs, his aunt offers to look after him. His mother objects, alleging that his aunt is a drug-user, a claim she denies.

Without agreement, Harold may be subjected to care proceedings if the social worker deems him to be 'at risk'. Avoiding this outcome could motivate the family into further discussions on how to support Harold and his mother. The social worker has several dilemmas to resolve: navigating through family disagreements; unpicking allegations of drug abuse; ensuring that whoever volunteers to look after Harold can care for him and affirm good behaviour; helping Cynthia avoid drugs; examining the impact of being a white working-class lad on his actions; and getting his views on any ensuing proposal. The values of empowerment, self-determination, human rights and harm reduction sit alongside resource availability when undertaking the next step.

Harold's human rights to be adequately looked after and enjoy family life have to be balanced with his becoming a law-abiding citizen. His mother's allegations have to be investigated carefully while not jeopardizing his aunt's human rights. The social worker has multiple roles and accountabilities to consider, and to this end can draw upon British law like the 2004 Children Act and the 1998 Human Rights Act, as well as international instruments such as the United Nations Convention on the Rights of the Child.

Conclusions

Social work is constantly changing as a result of economic constraints, political interventions, legislative initiatives, professional considerations and service user demands. Social workers work in a vast array of contexts and settings, with groups of people who cover the complete life cycle and cross ethnicities, cultures and abilities. This heterogeneity makes social work difficult to define and can confuse the public, who often wonder what they do, especially if things go wrong, as occasionally occurs, or a child's life is endangered. Social workers enhance people's well-being by enabling them to function more adequately, acquire the resources to do so and seek both personal and organizational change in the process. Social workers have to maintain individual rights in extremely trying circumstances and retain a sense of balance and purpose, even if taking tough decisions that deprive individuals of their liberty. Social workers are more likely to receive a bad press than other professions, even if the work they do is more complex and less amenable to easy solutions.

What social workers do is appreciated for its practicality. Service user satisfaction is reward for doing the work well. Nevertheless, what social workers do and how they do it is contested within the profession and outside it. The ensuing debates raise legitimate concerns about what constitutes their job. A long-standing unresolved issue entails their involvement in transformational social change that alters the balance of power between people and the nature of social relationships.

2

Working with Children, Young People and Their Families

Child Saviour or Child Snatcher?

Children represent society's future. Key aspects of professional social work are practitioners' interventions orientated towards: enhancing children's well-being; ensuring that they grow up in healthy and safe environments; and developing their full potential. Social workers work with children who truant from school and young offenders. They also help parents to: look after children and obtain resources for solving problems associated with poor parenting skills; use existing resources effectively; and find accommodation. However, as these services are seen as residual, the public perceives social workers' help as stigmatizing. Social workers' aim to meet 'the best interests of the child' is governed by two demands: promoting children's well-being and safeguarding them from harm. One would expect that in a society that values children, responses to the former would exceed the latter. In practice, the opposite is the case. Protecting children from harm comprises the bulk of statutory social work and takes resources away from preventative work that could promote child well-being.

Investigating allegations of child abuse – physical or emotional neglect, physical violence and sexual assaults perpetrated against children – has become central to protective work in safeguarding children and is underpinned with tight legislative and procedural controls. Known as child protection, it constitutes a large proportion of social workers' caseload. In these situations social workers seek to balance risks with needs. Child protection investigations of alleged child abuse overwhelm workloads, disproportionately attract available resources to skew allocations in their favour, and impede social workers' capacity to engage in preventative activities. Safeguarding children is a stressful area of practice because practitioners have to balance the rights of children with those of adults, including when investigating alleged child abuse. As many of these allegations prove to be unfounded, social workers face hostility from members of a child's family for doing investigative work that could disrupt family relationships.

At this point, the social worker as child saviour can become the child snatcher. Birth parents are suspicious of social workers' power to remove children if they negatively evaluate parental capacities and care-giving. Violence against social workers is not unknown in these and other circumstances. Some have been murdered, e.g., Ashleigh Ewing in 2006. Many will not conduct home visits or go to a child's home unless accompanied by another worker or the police. Worker safety is an issue in both the office and service users' homes. Social workers are trained to defuse potentially violent situations and use risk assessments in taking measures to ensure their own safety. Risk assessments are used to determine the likelihood that a person will harm another and what actions might be taken to prevent the likelihood of such harm coming to pass. Concerns that social workers' safety is being compromised have led to risk assessments now being used to assess the likelihood of harm befalling both social workers and service users and workers.

In this chapter I examine the care–control dilemmas that social workers address when working with children, young people and families – what works and what does not in 'looking after the best interests of the child'. I use case vignettes to highlight the tensions parents experience in relating to social workers, who have the power either to 'save' their children or to 'take them away'. These include examples in which young people have truanted from school and high-profile cases of child abuse emphasized in recent public inquiries like that into the murder of Victoria Climbié. In these, I show how difficult social circumstances affect parenting potential, restrict the options that poor parents can exercise and limit the nature of social work intervention in such cases. I show how work with children can benefit from beginning where the child is at and creating supportive systems like play therapy to achieve child safety in abusive contexts.

Contemporary Children's Services in the UK

Working with children, young people and families is reflected in the organizational structure of local authorities. Practice in this area is subject to constant change to improve outcomes for children, with legislation, organizational structures and agency arrangements outlining the direction of travel. The fragmented services and specialist agencies that featured in British social work after World War II disappeared with the Seebohm restructuring of the 1970s. This created social services departments as large bureaucratic empires that placed different areas of practice – children, older people, disabled people, young offenders, users of mental health services – under one directorship. Though never fully implemented, the unitary, one-stop shop based in the community was advocated in the Seebohm (1968) Report, echoed in the Barclay (1982) Report and endorsed by generic training. Dissatisfaction with current arrangements led to the transformation of social services being placed on New Labour's modernizing agenda. It aimed to improve the quality of services, worker efficiency, user involvement in service delivery and public confidence in the system (DH, 1998).

A winning formula for restructuring services has proved elusive, despite many overhauls of the child protection system. The most recent after the Laming (2003) Report has an agenda for change espoused in *Every Child Matters* (DfES, 2004). The 2004 Children Act sought to promote the aims of *Every Child Matters: The Green Paper* (DH, 2003) and create universal and unstigmatized services for children. *Working Together to Safeguard Children* (DfES, 2006) epitomizes the modernization agenda and government's wish to safeguard and promote children's welfare. Fragmented services remain a key problem, although the post of Minister for Children was created in 2005 to oversee the development of effective children's services throughout the country. Margaret Hodge, first in this office, proved a controversial figure. She did not enjoy the confidence of professionals active in the field, thus limiting her impact. As of this writing (July 2008), the position of Minister for Children, Young People and Families is occupied by Beverley Hughes. (The DfES was reorganized in June 2007 to become the Department for Children, Schools and Families, or DCSF.) Professor Sir Albert Aynsley-Green was appointed the first Commissioner for Children in England in 2005 to promote children's welfare, listen to their voices, respond to their issues and develop services. Children's Commissioners had been appointed in Scotland, Wales and Northern Ireland earlier. Local Area Committees

(LACs) oversee overall provisions in a geographical area and ensure the availability of the services required. Investigations into what life is like for young people in an area and local authority support for them are conducted by Local Area Reviews (LARs). In theory, these aim to help practitioners evaluate their interventions. These structures are being overtaken too.

Social services departments have been split into children's services and adult ones, generating new organizational structures for contemporary social work. There is no fixed national grand plan, but adult services are mainly linked to health; children and family services to education. This restructuring seeks to reshape service provision for children and families, foster social inclusion and cooperation between different agencies and make children's directors responsible for children's services. In addition, it tackles overlaps between social work and relevant activities in education, health, housing and youth services by bringing them together. They are to work as an integrated service using a single assessment and identification, referral and tracking system and national children's database (DH, 2002c).

Local authorities have scope to find local solutions to the latest reorganization. They are assisted in delivering children's services by agencies in the private and voluntary sectors and professionals in health, education, the criminal justice system and police services. The National Society for the Prevention of Cruelty to Children (NSPCC), with a long history of supporting statutory social workers, is also involved in these arrangements. The wealth of service providers has broadened the range of employers. But it requires excellent coordination for agencies not to work at cross-purposes or duplicate efforts. Child protection case conferences, often coordinated by social workers, bring all professionals involved with a child around a table to symbolize integration and discuss care plans. Despite such endeavours, however, differences in organizational cultures and difficulties in coordination and communication between agencies persist.

Children's Trusts represent another attempt at integrating fragmented services. Developed in 2003 as Pathfinder Trusts, these were managerial arrangements to coordinate and pool resources in caring for children in 35 chosen locales. These became Children's Trusts in 2006 to bring together local services for children and young people living in a specific geographical area and improve outcomes. All areas are intended to have Children's Trusts delivering integrated children's services by the end of 2008. Practitioners employed by Children's Trusts have a degree of local autonomy, but are to: operate within the *Common Assessment Frame-*

work (CAF) (DH, 2000); practise within integrated processes; share outcomes that can be assessed through performance management; and be rewarded individually according to performance. Professionals are to: listen to children; work on joint needs assessments; share decisions about priorities; identify all resources in an area; develop joint plans for deploying them; and work under a strong leader. This might not be a Director of Social Services and its potential absence is a major departure from the Seebohm reorganization.

Children's Trusts are charged with supporting professionals who work with children and tackling cultural and professional divisions so that their work can be integrated effectively into a team operating as one. Ofsted (Office for Standards in Education) can use a Joint Area Review (JAR) which occurs at the same time as a Corporate Assessment (CA) of a local authority to ensure that agencies form integrated organizations working to a national framework and capable of delivering local services, as specified in the 2004 Children Act. The Children and Young Persons Bill, debated in the House of Lords in early 2008, foreshadows further significant changes in social work. It might: introduce the outsourcing of social work services for 'looked after' children to private agencies; allow young people to remain in care until 18 (currently 16); require children and young people to be placed in their local area; require a statutory review before a child can be moved from an existing placement; and provide care leavers at university with an additional £2000 bursary. Private social work care practices will continue to be monitored by Ofsted under tougher powers and trialled as pilots before being extended countrywide.

Children's Safeguarding Boards are replacing Area Child Protection Committees. Social workers may now work for a Children's Services Trust rather than a local authority and provide packages of support and guidance in an independent Family Support Children's Centre. These centres offer support groups, training in parenting skills and monitor those using their holistic services. Family support will gain greater priority through the formation of 3500 Children's Centres by 2010. The notions of extended schools and 'wrap-around' care are to assist these processes by placing early intervention and education at their heart and helping parents get into the labour market.

The British government's preventative thrust regarding children is currently located in 'early years' interventions, which include Sure Start, an initiative to prepare children under 5 for a better start in life, especially in education. These projects help young children prepare for schooling and receive appropriate parenting and health care. Those running Children's Trusts are expected to liaise with Sure Start for young children, Connexions and other youth organizations for older children and teenagers. Sure Start, based on America's Headstart, targets young mothers and children to pre-empt educational problems. It has had mixed research results over long-term effectiveness in lifting children out of poverty. Neither initiative addresses the structural problems parents face, – poverty, low incomes, poor long-term employment prospects or bad housing. Thus, their positive impact has been limited.

Parenting under the Social Worker's Gaze

Family life is a complicated business and there are diverse opinions about how best to raise children. Social workers become implicated by being responsible for upholding family forms endorsed through legislation and social norms. There are differences of opinion about what constitutes a family, with some models having more sway than others. In Western capitalist societies like Britain, the white heterosexual nuclear family is the yardstick for measuring all others, enshrined in legislation and supported through the benefits system. Those who diverge from this may be tolerated, but they are considered aberrations from the norm and often penalized (Strega et al., 2002).

The work mothers do in raising children has been termed 'mother-work'. Most social work interventions in families occur through the mother, who is expected to 'protect the children from harm'. Her 'failure to protect' can result in children being taken into care (Strega, 2004). This dynamic forms the crux of gender relations in the child protection system, with mothers being offered support and placed under surveillance to ensure they meet required standards of care. These are usually associated with white middle-class mothering. Those labelled 'good' or 'deserving' parents/mothers comply with white, heterosexual middle-class norms – a mother and father of different genders and two children. 'Bad' or 'undeserving' parents/mothers have multiple problems, live in poverty and cannot adequately care for children. On the other side of the dichotomy, 'good' parents provide for and raise children satisfactorily.

A 'deserving' parent can become a 'good' one by responding appropriately to social work support. This takes a variety of forms, depending on a practitioners' assessment of parental capacity in raising children and reacting effectively to their interventions. A parenting assessment is a tool for evaluating parental capacity to care for or harm a child. A social worker completes a 'risk assessment' to determine the likely risk of a child being harmed (Woodcock, 2003). Deserving parents constantly have to prove they are worthy of support. A group of researchers investigating young mothers with children in care in Canada have theorized this as 'looking promising' (Rutman et al., 2002; Strega et al., 2002; Callahan et al., 2003; Dominelli et al., 2005). One practitioner clarifies the link between being defined as a parent who 'looks promising' and receiving resources by commenting that if a young mother is

> an active parent, a cooperative parent, a good parent then . . . I'll go to my manager and I would support that [request] and that'll happen.

The young mothers saw it as a game of constant surveillance and jumping through hoops to prove their parenting capacities. As one stated:

> If you chose to keep your child, you're stuck trying to prove yourself to your social worker. It doesn't matter how supportive my social worker was. I still have to prove to her that I was doing a good job.

Young mothers in this research project wanted to 'break the cycle' of bad parenting they had experienced as children. They thought that their own children's life chances would be enhanced if they were supported adequately to take care of them rather than surrender them to state care (Dominelli et al., 2005). A number of practitioners concurred with this view because they felt that policymakers had no inkling of the real problems faced by young mothers on low incomes who could not afford to feed their babies or provide for their intellectual development. The Canadian state responded to some of these critiques by providing resources for children who were in care past the arbitrary leaving age of 19 and supporting those in full-time education to finish their studies. In 2008, Britain considered raising the age of support for 'looked after' children from 16 to 18.

Parents whose parenting skills are found wanting – the 'bad' or 'undeserving' parents – are unlikely to receive social work support. They fall into the category that cannot be helped. Their children are taken into care, now termed 'looked after' or 'accommodated' children in British social work parlance. Once in care, children may be sent to foster parents on a temporary basis, be put up for adoption if a permanent solution is deemed necessary, or be placed in a residential institution of some sort.

The seemingly inclusive gender-neutral language of parenting disguises raising children as work that mothers, not fathers, do. Fathers are not configured as prime carers because fathering is associated with the biological act of being a sperm donor and economic act of providing financially for a family, while mothering is linked to the social processes of raising children. In child protection, parent is a substitute word for mother. Leaving fathers out of the loop can render invisible their contributions to child care. Social workers rarely work directly with fathers unless they have sole custody, usually when the mother is unavailable or deemed 'unfit'. Fathers in these situations are expected to undertake the 'motherwork' with children.

'Looked After' Children

'Looked after' children are taken into care for a variety of reasons. These include: the absence of parents, often through illness; parents' inability to care for them; and offences committed by children. Children are taken into care under the rubric of looking after the 'best interests' of the child. What this phrase means is contested, depending on who is doing the defining. Generally, it is assumed to mean ensuring the well-being of the child in all its dimensions. The Department of Health (2003) has defined well-being as being 'healthy, safe, enjoying and achieving in life, making a positive contribution to family and society and achieving economic well-being'. Parents' views of its meanings may differ from those expressed by social workers. It can become very problematic if social workers think that the best interests of the child are served by his or her removal from the parental home while parents are adamant that, whatever their shortcomings, they are best equipped to look after them. Social workers' opinions in these matters are determined by their assessment of the mother's and/or father's capacities as parents. If these parents' capacities are judged poor and inappropriate, a social worker can invoke the statutory removal of children and take parents to court to ensure that their assessment has legal backing. In this court hearing, parents and the child can have legal representation to challenge social workers' views of their parenting skills. In England, Guardians are appointed to support children through care proceedings and processes. If endorsed by the court, social workers' opinions supersede the parents'. CAFCASS (the Children and Family Court Advisory Service), formed in 2001 when the probation service lost this role, supports families in divorce proceedings and works to the 'best interests' of the child.

Specific legislation guides social workers' actions with children in most countries. Social workers have to know which piece of legislation applies in a given situation, although they can get specific advice from lawyers attached to their agency. The latest in the UK is the Children Act 2004. The UK had 92,400 children under 'corporate' care provided by substitute families or residential institutions in 2004. Of these, 65 per cent were fostered. The phrase 'corporate parent' covers a range of institutional parenting arrangements endorsed by the state for 'looked after' and 'accommodated' children under state care. The state may discharge its responsibilities through substitute families (fostering and adoptive) or residential care in private, voluntary or state agencies. The statutory sector retains responsibility for monitoring outcomes and ensuring that standards are maintained.

The 2004 Children Act replaced the 1989 Children Act, which consolidated previous legislation relating to children's welfare and introduced consideration of a child's cultural, religious and ethnic needs. Black practitioners and others lobbied for the inclusion of these in the 1989 Act to address serious deficiencies in state care of black children. The New Black Families Unit, the Soul Kids Campaign, Black and In Care and the Association for Black Social Workers and Allied Professions (ABSWAP) were formed to improve practice with black children and find black foster carers (Small, 1987; Dominelli, 1997; Graham, 2006). Under the 1989 Children Act, children in the UK were 'looked after' (formerly taken into care) by local authorities by being accommodated under Section 20 on a voluntary basis or subject to a Care Order on a statutory (mandatory or court-ordered) basis: 31 per cent to 65 per cent, respectively.

Parents are encouraged to enter voluntary arrangements, because these give them greater scope to influence what happens to the child and are less expensive to implement as they do not require formal court hearings. Parents request voluntary accommodation to address specific circumstances like a mother's illness or a child's behaviour that is difficult to control. Social workers can seek Emergency Protection Orders (EPOs) if parents threaten to withdraw children from voluntary arrangements and they consider this move harmful. Social workers may place children in substitute families (foster parents) or residential care in institutions designed for the purpose for specified periods. Policy currently favours fostering and adoption over residential care for children requiring permanent solutions. Residential provisions can be inadequate and expensive, often costing around seven times more than foster care.

By accommodating children, the state assumes the role of parent to the children in their care, and grandparent to any of their children in turn (Dominelli et al., 2005). The capacity of the state to act as parent or grandparent to different generations of children in the same family has been questioned because the outcomes for these children are often poor. Those who are 'looked after' are over-represented amongst disadvantaged children. They are more likely to: be excluded from school; truant; be involved in offending behaviour; participate in low-paid work; be unemployed; and experience mental ill health (Fleming et al., 2005; Stanley, 2005).

The law enjoins social workers to treat all parents equally, but parental rights are differentially applied in practice. This is partly due to social workers' stereotypes and concerns about the parenting abilities of certain types of parents. For example, black children in Britain and aboriginal children in Canada are over-represented in the care system because social workers do not trust parents sufficiently to look after their children. Their different child-rearing practices and attitudes to life are deemed 'risky' or deficient and pathological when measured against the white middle-class yardstick that defines parental norms in child welfare. Working within this stance, social workers minimize risk or anticipated likelihood of harm by 'rescuing' children from parents by taking them into care, where, in theory, better parenting is available.

The age and ethnicity of both parents and children are not the only consideration that practitioners take into account in determining risk. Parental substance misuse is also important. A mother who abuses drugs or alcohol when pregnant can lose a child at birth if deemed an 'unsuitable' parent. If social workers fear that a woman is unable to care for her body properly during pregnancy, she may be taken to court and ordered to look after herself in specified ways to protect the health of the forthcoming child. This occurred to Mrs G, a Gitxsan woman in Canada in the late 1990s, to prevent extensive damage to child health and development linked to Foetal Alcohol Syndrome (FAS). Young mothers of First Nations descent are disproportionately associated with FAS and subjects of such orders, despite professional misgivings about depriving women of control over their bodies. Another problem with such interventions is that they focus on maternal inadequacy and ignore contributory factors that are structural, e.g., poverty, physical, sexual and emotional abuse, and, for aboriginal women, the experiences of colonization in residential schools where they were abused and denied their culture. Similar hazards arise in the UK, as the case below indicates.

Case study: Social work involvement with a mother who misuses substances

Regina, a woman from Eastern Europe, married a white English man and came to live in the UK just before the fall of the Berlin Wall. She found living in England tough. It was difficult to make friends. Her qualifications as a doctor were not recognized and she took a job stacking shelves at a local supermarket. Her husband, a seaman, was away a lot and she felt isolated, lonely and useless. She began to drink heavily and ended up losing her job. This made her drink even more, although she managed to hide the extent of her drinking from her husband. She also took drugs when she could. When pregnant, she refused to see a doctor and spent much of the day in bed. When their son, Mark, was born in hospital, he was severely underweight and identified as having severe Foetal Alcohol and Substance Disorder (FASD) and placed in intensive care.

Social workers, health workers and drug workers were called in to work with Regina as a team to get her off alcohol and drugs and so that she could learn how to take care of Mark. When the baby finally came home, Mark and Regina were monitored closely. Mark's condition meant that he needed a lot of attention and cried constantly. Regina found this stressful and began drinking again and trying to hide it. Meanwhile Mark's growth and development were extremely slow.

Social workers accommodated him in voluntary foster care and worked with Regina and her husband, helping them take responsibility for parenting the baby by allowing him home under close monitoring on weekends when the father was there. The approach was tried with various permutations for nearly a year, at which point the social worker decided Mark needed permanency, with adoption by a white English family. A court sanctioned this plan despite parental opposition.

Regina's case exposes the way in which racist practices outside the family can impact on children, e.g., lack of recognition for overseas qualifications and social isolation for those who are different. Children are entitled to their cultural heritage and own sense of identity, but Mark's dual heritage was ignored. The 1989 Act (Sec. 22(5)) requires that the ethnic grouping and cultural traditions of 'looked after' children are considered. Safeguarding a child's identity does not mean treating it as fixed and immutable or essentialized. Social workers should explore the meaning of identity for a particular child and not assume that it is homogeneous and unitary and that those sharing an identity are all the same. In the fluid processes of identity formation, social workers have to balance continuities in children's sense of who they are with their desire to establish their own identities as they grow up.

The 1989 Act required local authorities to provide for the needs of *all* children living within their jurisdiction, regardless of status, in a brave attempt to de-stigmatize services associated with those having 'special' needs. These provisions of the Act have never been fully funded or enacted, so the goal remains to be met. Social work interventions primarily target those most 'in need' or 'in danger of being harmed' to cope with limited resources allocated to meeting children's welfare needs. Social workers use Section 17 for children 'in need' and Section 47 for those 'in need of protection from significant harm'. Defining a child as one or the other is crucial in accessing resources, as different services are available under each section. Issues of low income should be addressed for children defined as 'in need' and considerations of safety guaranteed for those 'in danger of being harmed'. In practice neither response is foolproof, and if interventions are misplaced or go wrong, social workers get into serious difficulty. Lisa Arthurworrey, responsible for looking after Victoria Climbié, lost her job for not protecting her. She saw her as being 'in need', without recognizing that she was already being harmed and 'in need of protection' too. Lisa Arthurworrey took her case to a Tribunal to challenge her exclusion from working with children for the rest of her professional life because not simply personal, but systemic. The Tribunal agreed and she was reinstated.

Social workers intervene in families to safeguard children. In a Western context that affirms family privacy, public intervention is stigmatizing and indicates parental failure. When intervening, social workers should ensure that they work in partnership with parents. To reduce parental anxieties, social workers should explain plans and actions to parents, taking them through court processes if necessary and being clear about the rationale underpinning the decisions they make on behalf of children. Parents do not lose their rights as parents simply because a social worker calls.

Social workers can refer families to other professionals for support. A range of support services, including those provided by children's centres, are available for this task and involve social workers in negotiating packages of care with different agencies. Inter-agency working and coordinating the contributions of several professional groups are key facets of work with children and families, and can encompass statutory, private and voluntary organizations. Examples of uses of the voluntary sector include a social worker using the NSPCC to support a sexually abused child or a probation officer asking a Victim Support worker to help a family traumatized by a robbery at home. Multi-agency working can be stressful for parents when they have to repeat stories over and over again to different professionals because they have not received or read their specific case-notes. One family in my research claimed that 25 professionals, ranging from health to probation, were supporting them. If communication between agencies is poor, it adds to work undertaken by parents as part of the 'motherwork' done by mothers.

Contentious Families

Diversity in family formations is becoming more acceptable. They are not all seen as equal. This affects social workers, as is shown by a case from Quebec, Canada, a country proud of its multiculturalism and tolerant attitudes towards difference.

Case study: Social worker involvement when identities are contested by the state

A group of Mennonites (a religious sect) moved from Manitoba to Quebec in the 1990s. They set up home in Roxton Falls, integrating into the society by finding jobs, making friends and speaking French. In 2007, Quebec authorities threatened to remove children from 15 families and place them in foster homes because their parents refused to send children to state-sanctioned schools. The Mennonites have their own school to teach children from Grades 1 to 7, enrolling eight children in 2006. But the teacher is not certified (accredited by the state) and Quebec's official curriculum is not being taught.

Mennonites reject the state curriculum for emphasizing evolution, lacking moral standards and accepting alternative lifestyles. Those with school-age children have threatened to move away. The mayor of Roxton Falls wants them to remain. But as education is a provincial matter, he is powerless to implement his wishes. He feels Mennonites

> are part of the community of 1,300. Losing 15 families would have a considerable economic and social impact on it. The Education Ministry says they must obey the law. It decrees the children be sent to state schools or private ones with specific classes to teach their religious views. Teachers in these private schools will still have to be certified and the school will need to have a permit to teach. Social workers will initiate care proceedings if agreement is not reached.

This case exemplifies conflict between: society's liberal values and its unitary sense of identity as a binding force endorsed through institutional power; and different layers of authority interacting with and impacting upon each other. The ethical dilemma posed is not as simple as the Ministry formulates it. Mennonites will have to teach a curriculum they find objectionable if the court rules against them (Riga, 2007). If they do not comply, social workers will remove the children from parental care.

Mormons in Bountiful, British Columbia, highlight other tensions between minority religious beliefs and dominant norms. A group of women, including social workers, have campaigned to charge Mormon men who marry children as young as 12 with child sexual abuse for having sex with minors, an offence in Canadian law. Their court case is pending, but social workers have taken some children from their parents in the meantime. Britain does not have significant numbers of these two religious groups, but the issue of parity between different religious traditions and English law is pertinent. Examples of these issues include: Jehovah's Witnesses' refusal of blood transfusions even if these might save a child's life; Catholics' views on abortion; and Sharia law's specific positions on women's reproductive rights, inheritance and entitlements to family property after divorce. These religious views, which sit uneasily with white British secular traditions, draw social workers into resolving disputes that affect the well-being of women and children.

Family life, sacred to religious groups, can conflict with women's rights as citizens if these have to be reconciled with patriarchal social relations that privilege men. This covers motherhood and employment, where women's rights as mothers remain unmet. For example, biological mothers in Canada combine parental and maternity benefits for a total of 50 weeks of paid leave, with 35 weeks from federal employment insurance and 15 weeks from maternity benefits from the unemployment insurance benefits system. Adoptive mothers can access only the first. In

2007, Patti Tomasson, an adoptive mother, alleged discrimination on these grounds and filed suit to access the additional 15 weeks of maternity benefits. Justice Mark Nadon, who heard the case in the Federal Court of Appeal, ruled that these provisions did not apply as 'she had not endured the physiological burdens of pregnancy and childbirth', claiming that '[e]xact parity between biological and adoptive mothers would result in discrimination . . . against biological mothers' (Rook, 2007: A6). She is appealing to the Supreme Court of Canada. This differential approach to adopted children is also experienced by British subjects. British parents living abroad cannot pass on British citizenship to adopted children like they can to birth children. If the children live abroad, British parents cannot claim child benefit. Social workers can advocate for state endorsement of rights in these cases.

Internationalized Social Problems

An international dimension in social work with children occurs on two main fronts – the sex trade and trafficking in children; and international adoptions. Unscrupulous dealers and middlemen have set up bogus adoption agencies or illegal foster homes from which to ply their trade and evade social workers' scrutiny and safeguards of children's rights. In one illustration, in 2007, 46 babies and young children were discovered for the American market in an illegal foster home in Guatemala. The USA now requires two sets of DNA tests to prove children are Guatemalan to bring adoptive parents under statutory control. The results are disappointing (Rosenberg, 2007). The US government has asked Guatemala to ratify the Hague Convention on Intercountry Adoptions to strengthen its adoption law and reduce American adoptions through unauthorized channels. The UN called for suspension of Guatemalan adoptions until this legislation came into effect on 1 January 2008. Illegal foster homes from which children are adopted remain, with gangs running them suspected of child trafficking. Similarly, in 2008, Zoë's Ark, a French charity bidding to 'rescue orphans' from poverty, was accused of trafficking children from Chad when their parents were identified.

Social workers in the UK and other parts of Europe have encountered difficulties with overseas adoptions when Western European adoptive parents have sought to bring home babies from Eastern Europe without following vetting procedures and obtaining social worker approval for these to take place. There are class, 'race' and ethnic dimensions to these sagas because adopters are well-off Westerners while the babies' mothers are poor and/or 'black', or those whose physical attributes are not White European. Celebrities 'rescuing' children from Africa expose class and racial inequalities as economic prospects and material advantages are pressed at the expense of children's identity and culture. What begins as a personal issue becomes a matter for social workers when safeguarding children's interests: for example, British social workers became responsible for ensuring that Madonna and Guy Ritchie upheld the 'best interests' of David Banda, including his cultural heritage, when he was adopted from Malawi.

Abused Children

Children can be subjected to different types of abuse, including physical or sexual abuse and neglect. Neglect is usually committed by women; men outnumber women in the other two categories. The physical abuse of children can result in death, with 50 children a year being killed by carers in the UK. In the most serious cases, statutory agencies have failed children by not preventing the deaths. Public inquiries are held to investigate what went wrong and propose changes in policy and practice. There were 70 such inquiries between the murder of Maria Colwell in 1973 and Laming's investigation into Victoria Climbié's death in 2000 (see case study below). Most recommend tackling failures in inter-agency working and improving communication amongst the different bodies involved in looking after a specific child. Rarely did they focus on the *causes* of tragic events within family relationships, including pressures that make those caring for children incapable of acting responsibly or safeguarding their well-being. Tackling these issues might produce greater progress in realizing children's growth and development. A further problem is the crisis intervention nature of work, which consumes resources needed for long-term preventative care.

Case study: Inter-agency failures in Victoria Climbié's death

Victoria Climbié was murdered in 2000 by her great-aunt and the woman's boyfriend after months of cruelty and ill treatment. She came to Britain from the Ivory Coast through France, where her parents initially sent her to advance her education and prospects for a better life. Victoria had been improperly documented, being passed off at border controls by her great-aunt as her daughter Anna. This misinformation was not picked up by immigration officials in either France or the UK. A Child at Risk Emergency Order that a French school had placed on Victoria was not transferred for monitoring in Britain, an omission that highlights the merit of developing cross-jurisdictional systems for sharing information. In the UK, Victoria was assessed by a number of professionals in the NHS, police, social services, education and NSPCC without her abuse being recognized. She had a black social worker whose white supervisors failed to support her adequately as they were unaware of the variety in black people's cultures.

The Laming Report into Victoria's death led to a massive restructuring of children's services and demands for social workers and other professionals to learn the lessons from this tragedy to protect other children from similar torture. It failed adequately to address issues of 'race' and racism or children's powerlessness. The absence of opportunities for children to voice concerns in situations of powerlessness is a crucial impediment to their ability to report or protest abuse by carers. This includes the need for translators to hear children's stories and pass these on to the social workers so that a child's own voice can be heard. For example, did Victoria speak English, given her birth in a French-speaking country?

Children have been seriously abused by carers in residential establishments. Between 1973 and 1990, the Pindown Regime in children's homes in Staffordshire (Levy and Kahan, 1991), Frank Beck's abuses in Leicestershire (Kirkwood, 1993) and the sexual abuse scandal in Clwyd (Waterhouse, 2000) exemplify pernicious forms of abuse undertaken by carers in institutions. There have been others, before and since. Pastoral care provided by religious leaders such as priests in Christian churches (Kennedy, 2000) and carers/educators of First Nations children in residential schools (Furniss, 1995) have also been subject to betrayals of trust where children were sexually abused by those responsible for their care. Researchers have indicated that about 4 per cent of foster carers have abused children. Sexual abuse is not limited to particular sects, creeds, ethnicities or genders. It can occur in any setting and be perpetrated by anyone. Social workers have to be constantly vigilant for signs of abuse amongst parents, carers and co-workers, to listen carefully to children who try to speak of ongoing or past abuse and to take measures to investigate and end it.

Child protection issues are complicated, and social workers perform a balancing act in negotiating and balancing the rights of children with those of adults. This task can be very demanding. No wonder child protection workers get stressed out! It is also a reason for high turnover amongst child welfare workers, with large numbers leaving child protection. Social workers who have qualified overseas have been drafted in to fill the gap, and bring overseas-trained practitioners to work with British-trained ones. Their recruitment has to be consistent with equalities legislation and should be supported by having appropriate systems in place to welcome people on arrival, induct them into their new jobs and support them for a number of years. This support has not been forthcoming. Its lack hinders the recruits' integration into their new homelands and offices (Devo, 2006). Social workers recruited from Zimbabwe by Birmingham City Council have felt the inadequacy of their welcome and mobilized through the Zimbabwean Social Workers' Association to pursue claims for better treatment after arrival. The removal of so many workers from their country of origins is having serious repercussions in their homelands. In Zimbabwe, most qualified social workers are now employed overseas, causing serious domestic shortages (Devo, 2006). The UK introduced a Social Care Code of Practice for International Recruitment in 2006 to improve the treatment of overseas workers. UK-based social workers can insist that recruitment policies and practices in their offices are anti-racist and conform to its provisions.

Children's entitlement to being cared for physically, emotionally and intellectually has been enshrined in national and international legislation, including various human rights acts and the 1989 United Nations Convention on the Rights of the Child (CRC), ratified by virtually all countries in the UN except the USA and Somalia. Article 19 of the CRC forbids the abuse of children. Its provisions are difficult to enforce, as individual nation-states have to allocate resources for this purpose. The CRC has moved towards accepting children as subjects in their own right. Adultism, or the sentiment that adults know what is best for children and can exercise power over them, remains a crucial dynamic in constructing contemporary childhood. Adultism persists at all levels, with children rarely making their own decisions. This places them in a position of dependency vis-à-vis adults and exacerbates their vulnerability. Providing children and young people with state-guaranteed incomes and the right increasingly to make their own decisions as they grow older could alleviate their dependent status.

Child welfare services have been criticized for not listening to children or taking seriously their views about what they want. Listening to them can highlight abuse. Children and young people have organized to get their voices heard. In Britain in the 1980s, the National Association of Young People In Care (NAYPIC) defined what constituted good residential care for children and young people. Black children formed the Black and In Care Group. Others groups include: Voice, Safe and Sound; Voices from Care; and Who Cares? Their demands that children and young people are involved in decisions made about them have been adopted by many projects, including the Lilac Projects in York and West Sussex during 2007. Young people are also active in the Youth Parliament, which allows young people to discuss issues of interest to them and then have dialogue with politicians, including members of the cabinet.

Sexually Abused Children

Substantial numbers of children are sexually abused. Sexual abuse involves the abuse of power over others and is not to be confused with non-abusive sexual relationships amongst peers. Researchers estimate that one in four girls and one in eight boys are abused by adults, often known to them and primarily by men. In working with children who have been sexually abused, social workers have to ensure that: they do not subject children and families to institutional abuse; they explain the procedures they will use; and they inform them of their rights. Institutional abuse occurs when an organization does not discharge its duty of care appropriately or as a deliberate act of exploitation. Children taken into care because they have been abused can experience institutional abuse if they are the ones removed from their homes, have to start school in another locale and make new friends. To reduce the impact of institutional abuse on children, feminists have demanded that the abuser be the one to leave. This proposal by feminists is problematic because the men are presumed innocent until proven guilty and their removal undermines this proposition. Thus, there has to be a general campaign of public education to ensure that being asked to leave their home does not lead to an automatic presumption of guilt.

Men and the few women convicted of sex offences against children are placed on a register for sex offenders. However, some professionals and members of the general public deem this an insufficient precaution and have called for additional measures to address their concerns that sex offenders are free to live as their next-door neighbours. The murder of a British child, Sarah Payne, who was sexually abused, led to calls for the passage of Sarah's Law, echoing the creation of Megan's Law in the USA after a young girl was murdered by a sex offender the police knew was living in the community. Megan's Law requires communities to be told when sex offenders come to live in an area. The British government refused to pass such legislation, since it felt that this would enable vigilante groups to dispense justice. Professionals can access the Sex Offender Register, and criminal record checks by the Criminal Records Bureau (CRB) are now required from those wishing to work with children and other vulnerable groups. However, these are unlikely to guarantee children's safety as many abusers lack a criminal record and are unknown to the police.

Adults sexually abused as children have begun to demand compensation for suffering and lost opportunities. After the Waterhouse Inquiry into allegations of abuse in Clwyd in Wales during the period 1974 to 1990, insurance companies who cover local authorities for such liabilities demanded that the results of abuse investigations not be published, for to do so, it was argued, would be to give lawyers taking these cases evidence to sustain their cause. This seems an outrageous proposition that deprives victim-survivors of their right to justice and knowledge of what happened to them whilst in care. Furthermore, it denies social workers the possibility of learning from mistakes made by others in not reporting or noticing abuse occurring in the workplace. Whistleblowing policies have been initiated to support such disclosures. Preliminary studies into their effectiveness, however, reveal that practitioners are reluctant to use these procedures (Clode, 2001).

Children can abuse other children if they have not addressed their own victimization and healed the damage it causes. Social workers can help them address their pain. Children in residential care can also be subjected to 'peer abuse', including sexual abuse and bullying by other children. This can occur if children who have been abused and those who abuse are placed in the same institution. This is an undesirable practice that cannot always be avoided as specialist places for children and young people are in short supply. If this occurs, the level of risk has to be calculated, protection plans have to be agreed and high levels of surveillance have to be maintained by staff as their presence acts as the greatest deterrent. Working with child sex offenders is difficult, challenging work. It requires specialist knowledge. One child in five has mental health issues. Psychiatric and psychological services are not always available to support children traumatized by abuse or if they have mental health problems. In England, comprehensive services are provided by multi-disciplinary teams known as Children and Adolescent Mental Health Services (CAMHS). Often based in NHS settings, these include social workers. Social workers, GPs and teachers can refer children to CAMHS.

Francesca St Pierre's death highlights institutional failings even if workers use risk assessment tools to develop individual safety plans, and it exposes how risk assessments and safety procedures do not offer the certainty of safety demanded of them.

Case study: Risk assessment tools and individual safety plans

Francesca St Pierre was 14 years old and had lived in a group home in eastern Montreal for three years 'for her own protection'. She had Tourette's Syndrome – a condition of multiple and severe tics requiring regular medication to control. She was allowed to go to school, participate in leisure activities and lead an independent life, riding her bicycle or the buses on her own, but subject to curfew. The young people in the home were supervised 24 hours a day, every day. Caregivers were carefully chosen to work with young people.

On the morning of Saturday, 18 August 2007, Francesca left the group home just after 11 to go to the library. She was expected back by noon. The care workers noticed that she was late and called the police at 1 o'clock to report her missing. Her badly battered body was discovered Sunday evening. Francesca had died as a result of a violent attack. A young lad in the group home was charged with her murder a few days later. (Cherry, 2007)

The staff at the group home had followed procedures to ensure Francesca had clear boundaries about her presence and absence from the home and knew what to do if she needed help. This case indicates shortcomings and potential dangers for children in risk assessments in a residential setting that can occur anywhere, including the UK. The safeguards were unable to protect Francesca from attack and eventual murder by a resident who had been bullying her. Her case suggests the importance of tackling bullying amongst peers, whether encountered at school, care homes or in families and not assuming that systems alone can guarantee a child's well-being. Promoting good relationships between service users is important too.

Conclusions

Working with children and families is both rewarding and stressful. Social workers hold enormous powers that they exercise 'in the best interests of the child'. They can disagree with parents about what is to be done, but they are likely to set the terms in disputes with them and have these upheld in court. This makes child welfare workers feared rather than welcomed into people's homes, as parents are wary of their children being removed ('looked after').

Nevertheless, the rewards of knowing that a child's life or well-being has been safeguarded and enhanced compensate for bleak moments when social workers feel besieged. Many children and young people have written to social workers to thank them for intervening in their lives in positive ways, as in this quote from a young mother:

> The last home that I ever lived in ... was the best. ... They were actually there for my support. They sat and listened to me when I felt the need to talk ... saying these are your choices ... which was good. I was never raised on choices ... they were very supportive of my culture. (cited in Dominelli et al., 2005: 1140)

Such responses make professionals feel their efforts have been worthwhile.

3

Working with Older People

Market-Driven Facilities or Universal Services?

Many individuals have more than one problem that social workers address, giving rise to the idea of multi-problem individuals or families. Poverty and bad housing are crucial issues for older people, especially for women living alone. These set the context for poor health and limited opportunities to enjoy a healthy, active old age and are differentiated according to 'race', gender, physical and mental capacities and sexual orientation. Older people may suffer from social isolation, require help in forming social networks around activities they can share with others, grieve the loss of loved ones and need bereavement counselling. Only a few call upon social services for help. Most look after themselves or are cared for by unpaid kin and neighbours in their own homes. A large proportion of older people contribute to other people's well-being by voluntary work, caring for those even older than themselves, supporting disabled people or looking after grandchildren whilst their parents do waged work.

Despite the positive contribution of older people to the social and economic life of a community, governments across the Western world, including the UK, are worried about an ageing population and assume this will impose a burden of care on younger sections of society. To address a potential shortage of institutional social care services and financial resources, governments propose care in the community. This chapter considers the rise, strengths and weaknesses of care management through community care as a key way of delivering services to older people.

Older People: An Under-Appreciated Group

The 2001 British Census indicated that 19.6 million people were aged over 50 compared to 16.0 million in 1961. Meanwhile, the percentage of under-16s dropped from 24 per cent to 20 per cent. Those in the 85-plus age rose fivefold to 1.1 million during this period. Black people over 50 numbered 672,000 in 2001, with those of Afro-Caribbean origins in the oldest profile. Black elders over 65 composed 6 per cent of the population and white elders 16 per cent. The Office for National Statistics estimated that there will be 1.7 million black elders by 2030. Despite these figures, only 5 per cent of all elders received social care (Lymbery, 2007); few were black.

Work with older people has traditionally been a Cinderella service – poorly resourced and performed largely by unqualified workers. Recent restructuring following the 2004 Children's Act split social services responsibilities into adult and children's social services to improve services and training in both. *Our Health, Our Care, Our Say* (DH, 2006) focused on improving community health and social care services and personalizing provision and delivery. A Director of Adult Services oversees services for older people, adults with mental ill health and learning-disabled people, and is responsible for safeguarding adults by protecting them from abuse and neglect.

Social work with older people occurs largely during times of crisis or transition. It is currently carried out by multi-disciplinary teams working in Primary Care Trusts (Ray and Phillips, 2002). These teams offer a 'seamless' service and determine need through the single assessment process defined in the National Service Framework for Older People (NSF) (DH, 2001a). Nigel Horner (2007) suggests that social worker involvement with older people had been negligible until research exposed their appalling care and Age Concern, Help the Aged and others campaigned for community care. He argues that care for older people moved from a 'medical' model that favoured hospitalization in the 1980s, to the 'institutional care' model that privileged care in a nursing home in the 1990s, to today's 'intermediate care' model. Intermediate care is to reduce need for hospitalization and keep older people at home. Mark Lymbery (2005) contends that the government's failure to define social workers' role in intermediate care releases opportunities to redefine practice with older people in more empowering directions.

In 2007, there were 611,000 people working in voluntary organizations; many with degree-level qualifications (NCVO and WH, 2007). Chris Phillipson (1982) claims that older people are seen as *un*important because they are no longer waged employees. Workers who care for them experience stigmatization by association (Parker, 2007a, 2007b). During the 1990s, the Warner (1992) Report and the Utting (1991) Report raised the issue of training residential care workers as a matter of urgency. Yet, 80 per cent of this workforce remains unqualified and works primarily in the social care sector. The government sought to address this problem by developing community care and supporting social care workers to train at National Vocational Qualification (NVQ) levels 2 and 3. However, these levels are lower than those obtained by qualified social workers, and this strategy has neither been adequately funded nor raised workers' status. It places women workers who staff these posts in a low-paid employment ghetto with limited prospects of developing high-status careers through the sector. 'Low-status service users, low-status workers' could be the maxim covering social care.

Community Care: Developing Packages of Care for Older People

The move towards community care for older people followed academic critiques, government reports and research that highlighted the appalling treatment of older people and suggested new ways forward. Key amongst these, the Griffiths (1988) Report, proposed: local authorities assume responsibility for the care of older people; social worker involvement; case managers to coordinate packages of care; and a 'mixed economy of care' to encourage private and voluntary providers alongside state ones. It ultimately laid the foundation for the National Health Service and Community Care Act (CCA) 1990. The Wagner (1988) Report also argued for community care as a positive choice promoting older people's dignity and quality of life.

The CCA 1990 produced the commissioner–provider split, a hallmark for community care today. Commissioning has promoted 'contract government', whereby the state purchases services from private and voluntary providers (Greer, 1994). The contracts entered into can be 'block', where government guarantees a certain amount of business that is fixed, or 'spot', where services are commissioned for an individual to give greater flexibility and choice. Commissioning has opened statutory services to the private and voluntary sectors in ways not seen since the formation of the welfare state in the 1940s, and it has ended statutory social services' brief reign as near-monopoly provider to promote a 'mixed economy of care'. The CCA 1990 legitimated social change through financial instruments rather than debates over political choices about services. This, Hoogvelt and I termed 'economics as ideology' (Dominelli and Hoogvelt, 1996).

Community care was a form of practice offering high-quality services to older people. Trialled in Kent under a generous funding regime during the 1980s, it showed that older people could be given more choice and be involved in determining the services that suited each of them (Challis and Davis, 1986). When introduced throughout the country as a poorly resourced service that relied mainly on private providers, the picture proved less rosy. This outcome raises political questions about whose responsibility it is to enhance personal well-being and where the necessary resources will come from. These issues lie at the heart of debates about the welfare state. They are currently answered in neo-liberal terms, i.e., individuals and families look after themselves with minimal state involvement. This stance counters the solidaristic social democratic one favoured when the British welfare state was set up after World War II. According to that approach, everyone pools resources to care for each other.

Private provision expanded when the Department of Health paid for services at fees demanded by the market. Rising prices made this approach unsustainable. When the state failed to fund services at market levels, many private providers pulled out from the residential sector, where from 1992 they had replaced local authority provision and shifted local authorities from monopoly supplier to provider of last resort. This development intensified the crisis in under-provision. The number of residential care homes in England dropped from 24,100 in 2001 to 21,000 in 2004. The private sector owns 71 per cent of them, the voluntary sector 17 per cent and local authorities 12 per cent. Together, they provide placements for 244,000 older people (ONS, 2005).

Social workers assess older people to identify their needs. They can use Section 47(1) of the CCA 1990 to challenge professional assessments, but may not get the resources they want if funds are short. A fundamental problem with the shift to local authorities is that elder care lost its universal (free) basis in the NHS and became a means-tested local authority provision targeting those most in need. Needs assessments became driven by resource availability and assessments became budget- rather than needs-led. Social workers became embroiled in reducing demands for services by tightening eligibility criteria and checking claimants' assets. Those owning a home are subject to a capital disregard of £21,500 (in 2007), whereby the value of their home above this limit is included in calculations used to pay for care. Some older people find this unfair as life savings invested in a home cannot be inherited by children. Eligibility frameworks now divide older claimants according to a hierarchy of needs: critical, substantial, moderate and low. Many local authorities meet only 'critical' needs. The interpretation of these criteria varies from one local authority to another. Consultation under *Fair Access to Care* (DH, 2002a) highlighted consistency in eligibility criteria, risk assessments, user charges and regular reviews of services as urgent priorities. The case study below indicates some of the moral dilemmas and difficulties that social workers experience when they cannot obtain the resources that will meet the needs of older people that they assess.

Case study: Ethical dilemmas for social workers working with older people

Elisabeth was a newly qualified social worker working as a care manager in a community care team in a not-for-profit agency. She was given her first caseload, which included a budget within which she had to work. She enjoyed working in this setting, getting to know older people and their families and arranging packages of care for them, involving them far as possible. The people she worked with thought she was 'a treasure'. She found working within stipulated budgets difficult, but was resourceful and managed to find means of getting what she needed through voluntary channels, seeking resources via the internet and chats with professionals she met at work.

She eventually reached the limits of her ingenuity. She had overspent her budget by a small amount when a referral for urgent respite care came in. Attempts to get help from the voluntary agencies she could access drew a blank. Her options were stark – she either turned the request down, even though the carer had been hospitalized for a period; she discharged another older person from respite care; or she waited for someone to die to release allocated funds. Elisabeth was distraught over these choices and could not reconcile herself to prioritizing the needs of these elders, as her manager advised. She spent a sleepless night trying to decide what to do. When she saw her manager in supervision the next morning, he told her that she 'had become *too* involved with her clients'. She did not deem this as fair comment and felt the responses to the service users and her were distorting the nature of the social work task. She did not have an answer to the question of providing for the needs of all those requiring help within her budget. She felt inadequate and wondered if this was the job for her. She returned to work the following day to hand in her notice.

The lack of resources and impact on staff morale highlighted by this situation is serious. Public spending in residential and nursing care for older people rose from £10 million in 1979–80 to £2 billion with the full implementation of community care in 1993 (Lewis and Glennerster, 1996). A Joseph Rowntree Report (Laing, 2004) claims that elder care has been under-funded by about £1 billion per year and is unable to reach the standards government set in April 2002. It predicts that spending on older people will have to increase by 315 per cent between 2000 and 2051 to meet the needs of older people. This will require the gross domestic product (GDP) expended on services for older people to rise from 1.4 per cent to 1.8 per cent during that time. Under-funding is a political issue. But, as Elisabeth's story reveals, it is difficult for social workers to focus on its political dimensions. They become embedded in the realities of day-to-day practice and focus on personal strengths and failings, as Elisabeth did. Instead of engaging in wider political issues that have to be sorted to deal effectively with their concerns, this approach drives them away.

The Sunderland (1999) Report aimed to improve the quality of care for older people. It argued for: free nursing and personal care in residential settings (accepted only in Scotland); a National Care Commission to monitor trends; sharing the costs of short-term and long-term housing, living expenditures and personal care between the public purse and person requiring care; and collaboration between health and social services under Best Value (DETR, 1998). As part of New Labour's modernization agenda, Best Value guides the commissioning framework and requires effectiveness, economy, efficiency and quality in the services delivered.

The National Service Framework for Older People (NSF) (DH, 2001) targets raising standards and quality in health and social care services. It addresses four themes:

- respecting the individual;
- intermediate care;
- providing evidence-based specialist care; and
- promoting an active, healthy life.

The NSF facilitates the delivery of integrated services and has eight standards:

- rooting out age discrimination;
- person-centred care;
- intermediate care;
- general hospital care;
- care during falls;
- stroke care;
- mental health and older people; and
- promotion of health and active life in older age.

The NSF promotes a single assessment process whereby quality assessments would identify individual needs. It identified four elements in the assessment process, namely:

- contact;
- overview;
- specialization around specific needs; and
- comprehensive levels of support for problematic needs and circumstances and intensive or prolonged treatment.

Although dominated by health experts, social workers can participate in all phases of the intervention process: health promotion; preventative services; primary care; community health services; social care; support for carers, including an assessment of their needs; and acute hospital care (DH, 2005). The role of social workers in the multi-disciplinary assessment process is far from clear, and a Review is under way to clarify this.

England's under-funded system of community care has been incapable of challenging the inadequacy of provisions for older people, the lack of priority given to their needs or those of their carers. This is despite the requirements to provide services for elders under the National Assistance Act 1948 or carers under the Carers (Equal Opportunities) Act 2004. Under-funding hinders practitioners' ability to comply with the National Service Framework for Older People and the National Minimum Standards for Older People of 2004. These aim to end age discrimination, and provide integrated services for and promote older people's health and well-being.

The gap between revenues and requirements in the UK is being covered by 6 million unpaid carers in the community. One-third of them are older people. Most are women. Community care has largely come to mean care by women, both as carers and as workers (Dominelli, 1997; Orme, 2001). Great pressure has been placed upon carers by inadequate support and funding. Significant numbers are experiencing depression and feel unable to continue (Moriarty and Levin, 1998). The increasingly bureaucratic nature of community care and care management for older people has shifted adult services from relational social work, where practitioners focus on helping relationships between them and service users, to delivering packages of care, where services are purchased under contract from voluntary and private providers.

Consumer Empowerment for Older People

The lack of say in services provided to older people has led to demands for change. Responses have covered: person-centred care; the extension of direct payments (DPs) to older people; and individual budgets (IBs). People aged over 65 became eligible for direct payments as part of the modernizing agenda (DH, 1998) in 2000. DPs are funds that local authorities pay to individuals so that they may purchase their personal care. Under this scheme, the older person purchasing services employs a personal assistant. The rules governing their use and the records that have to be kept regarding disbursement are complicated. The older person becomes an employer who pays tax and national insurance on employees' earned income directly to the Inland Revenue. Older people requiring help in understanding and completing the relevant forms can ask social workers to assist them. Cecilia's case study below evidences confusion in their use. Take-up was and remains slow, yet, despite this, in 2003 the government required local authorities to offer direct payments to all those receiving community care services.

Case study: Purchasing personal help

Cecilia, a 76-year-old white English woman, lived in social housing in a run-down inner city in northern England. She had reduced mobility as a result of arthritis since her early 50s and had had several adaptations to her bath to cope with her condition. In her late 60s, she had had several mild strokes that had left her slightly paralysed on the left side and she showed early signs of Alzheimer's. She lived on her own in the house she had shared with her husband until he died five years ago. Since then, she had looked after herself with some input from Ben, a neighbour aged 68, who did shopping and minor housework for her. Cecilia claimed she used direct payments to pay Ben, but could be confusing this with other funds because he is not her personal assistant.

Some service users see direct payments as medical and functional and prefer individual budgets. Funds for individual budgets (currently being piloted) are allocated from several funding streams and draw upon individual support plans that identify what is required and priorities across a wide range of needs. Individual budgets allow people to 'shop around' for best buys and cheaper workers to meet their care needs. Direct payments and individual budgets are popular for empowering users to gain financial control and choice in the services they purchase. These will alter social workers' roles, driving them to support older people in care planning and keeping financial records. In December 2007, Alan Johnson, Secretary of State for Health, announced the *Putting People First Vision* to: bring together central and local government bodies funding older people's services more effectively; orientate resources and practice to 'prevention, early intervention and re-enablement'; expand power, choice and control of service users and carers; and build aspects of individual budgets praised by people in the 13 sites piloting these. The vision was allocated £520 million for implementation.

Elder Abuse

The media, politicians and practitioners depict older people as a vulnerable and dependent client group. Their image as burdens and incapable of self-care understates their capacity for self-initiated social action to protect their interests. Older people have challenged this picture through self-care and social movements that they have organized and run, e.g., the British Pensioners and Trade Union Association and Action on Elder Abuse in the UK and the Townsendites and Gray Panthers in the USA.

The British Pensioner and Trade Union Association was formed in 1972 to take up issues and demand legislative change, 'justice and dignity in retirement'. One of their key concerns has been the 40,000 unnecessary deaths of older people caused by lack of money to buy fuel and other essentials because state pensions are set at abysmally low levels for those without occupational pensions. The Action Network has similar aims and campaigns vigorously for older people. Through activism, older people have created their own demands – rescinding a mandatory retirement age; decent pensions; buying their own care services; living in homes that enable them to retain links with community, friends and relatives; and a healthy, active old age. Social workers support such initiatives and work in agencies like Primary Care Trusts, Age Concern and Help the Aged.

Older people, like other citizens, worry about being harmed by con artists, some pretending to be social workers, who force themselves into their homes under the pretext of helping them. Other examples cover deliberate acts of violence during a burglary or 'home invasion'. Older people may be confused about what is happening. If experiencing dementia, they may resist attempts to help regardless of whether the source of assistance is a social worker, family member, friend or neighbour. Their desire to be independent also makes them reluctant to accept social workers' help.

Some older people, especially those with dementia or Alzheimer's disease, can become vulnerable as their mental and physical abilities deteriorate through these conditions and they become dependent on carers. The imperative here is for practitioners to work within older people's levels of decision-making to enhance their quality of life and capacities to engage actively with the world around them. Unscrupulous carers can abuse them in such situations, financially, emotionally and/or physically. Sometimes all of these forms of abuse may apply in a given case. An infamous instance of elder abuse was the murder of 250 older patients by the GP Harold Shipman between 1971 and 1998, who abused their trust and murdered them to appropriate their material assets. In another example, the National Care Standards Commission found the husband and wife GP team in charge of the Maypole Nursing Home in Birmingham guilty of elder abuse by not caring adequately for older people living there and causing 28 to die in one year (BBC News, 2003a). The charges were serious – the family of one man who died (Leslie Vine) requested a judicial review in August 2006 – and the home was closed. Elder abuse can also occur at the hands of trusted individuals, such as close relatives, as in the following case study.

Case study: Elder abuse by trusted individuals

Marge had been an active adult who had thought about deteriorating physical and intellectual capacities in old age and had taken measures to address this. She gave her only son, Tom, power of attorney over her financial affairs if she should need it. She got on well with him and this act gave her peace of mind. The arrangement worked well for years while Marge enjoyed full health. But, unknown to her, Tom had begun to abuse drugs. When Marge had a serious stroke that left her brain-damaged and paralysed, she became reliant on him to look after her affairs. Initially scrupulous about not using his mother's money for drugs, Tom lost his sensitivity after several years and began drawing on her funds to feed his habit. Eventually, he exhausted these, and when it came time for Marge to use her money to adapt the house, there was none left in her bank account. The issue came to light when her social worker did an assessment of her needs and assets (income and resources). Marge was devastated when the social worker told her the news. She felt deeply betrayed by the one person whom she had trusted and found the matter both distasteful and incomprehensible.

Marge's situation reflects the lack of social work intervention in the lives of older people unless there is a crisis requiring public attention. This occurred when Marge was due to leave hospital to prevent 'bed-blocking' by releasing the bed for another patient, as the doctors thought she no longer needed medical expertise. Social workers and doctors can disagree over when this point is reached as the decision is often made on budgetary rather than medical grounds. The issue hinges on whether social services or the NHS pays the bill for the person's care. The Commission for Social Care prioritized pressure for beds over the long-term needs of older people in 2004. Financial penalties can be imposed for bed-blocking, and this limits social workers' willingness to stand up for older people if medical practitioners remain adamant that they move out. In Marge's case, there was pressure on the social worker to accede to the doctor's definition of her readiness to leave hospital because delaying the discharge would trigger a penalty payment from social services under Section 2 of the 2003 Community Care (Delayed Discharges) Act. The question of 'Who pays?' becomes a budgetary device that can intensify professional rivalries. The position is somewhat surreal, since both sources of money come from the public purse – the taxpayers, who at one time included the older person contributing via a waged income. Older people continue to pay taxes like VAT on consumption when they purchase items.

Marge's situation was a disaster waiting to happen, and it underscores the importance of social workers not operating on stereotypical assumptions simply because they are pressured into finding fixed solutions to a problem. In Marge's case, this would have been to get her out of hospital quickly and free up the bed for another individual. Marge would have been discharged from hospital into the care of her son, except that her circumstances were fully investigated by the social worker. The care assessment exposed Tom's drug habit, financial abuse and betrayal of trust. Without such an assessment, the social worker would have assumed a 'normal' relationship between mother and son, with the son looking after his mother. But Tom could barely meet his own care needs. Marge's vulnerability can be seen as exposing both personal and structural failings. Tom has to be held accountable for stealing his mother's money. At the same time, society cannot be absolved of its neglect of people who misuse drugs by leaving them to be preyed upon by ruthless criminals operating a market in drugs; or its responsibility to care for elders, who are key constituents of society.

The Safeguarding Vulnerable Groups Act, which came into effect in 2006, with full implementation scheduled for October 2008, introduces a centralized vetting and barring scheme for people working with children and vulnerable adults. It extends vetting scrutiny to more sectors of the workforce than those currently used, to include those: providing training, instruction, teaching, treatment, therapy or interactive communications services; driving vulnerable people; managing service providers; and offering direct services and support workers for vulnerable people. Four existing lists – the PoCA List under the Protection of Children Act 1999; the PoVA List under the Care Standards Act 2000 for vulnerable adults; List 99; and the Disqualification List – will come under a unified Vetting and Barring Scheme (VBS) with a Children's Barred List and Adults' Barred List. An Independent Barring Board (IBB) will maintain the VBS to form a single register of all those working with children or vulnerable adults. The IBB has three options in barring people: automatic listing; automatic inclusion on the list; and discretionary listing. The first allows no representation and takes immediate effect. The second allows representation after a name is listed. A discretionary listing allows individuals to question being placed on the list before their name is added. Anyone who is on the barred list cannot register as a worker and is thus unable to work with vulnerable groups. Non-conviction information shared amongst agencies can facilitate the identification of child murderers like Ian Huntley by exposing allegations that have not been proven. The Act places the onus to register on individuals, not employers. A crucial weakness is that it does not cover family members caring for each other.

Contemporary Trends in Caring for Older People

Social workers can be hired by a variety of employers in the statutory, commercial for-profit, non-profit and voluntary sectors. Each employer has a different remit, but has a common value base in caring for vulnerable people. There are transferable skills, overlapping responsibilities and duties that may be found in each sector, e.g., promoting the well-being of individuals, families, groups or communities and initiating personal change. What is done and how it is done can differ substantially from one sector to the other. The user groups that each agency identifies as its own can vary considerably. For example, commercial for-profit firms looking for opportunities to make money are unlikely to be interested in heavy-end child protection issues, seriously disturbed individuals or even long-term chronically ill older people because they would be worried about their profit margins. Such establishments are likely to dip in and out of service provision, as happened in the UK during the 1990s when the government capped spending on private residential care for older people because it had become too expensive. The number of places in care homes has declined by 13 per cent since 1996, while the percentage of the population of the over-60s and over-85s has risen and is expected to peak in 2031.

The government is attempting to improve services for older people and advocating that 'every older person matters' to parallel its drive on 'every child matters'. Care Minister, Ivan Lewis, took the lead in demanding that support for family members caring for older people was strengthened, care standards rose and older people were treated with dignity. Shaun Woodward MP (2008: 22) quotes him as stating that:

> In the same way that the Children's Plan will shape the future of our country, the way we treat older people will determine its character. This year will see the most radical shake-up of older people's services for a generation.

Conclusions

Older people constitute an important group in need of social care services, but a socially under-valued one. Their carers are similarly under-appreciated. Most of them are women. State care is required by only a small proportion of older people. Social workers operate within strictly defined legislative parameters in delivering services to them and are held accountable for their work through bureaucratic management systems and the general public. The demands made of them by older people cover a gamut of needs from the physical to the psychological, from the financial to the social. The resources needed to provide the highest standards of care for all those in need are lacking, despite constant legislative changes to enhance service provision.

Older people want to live a healthy, active old age as far as possible. Any future arrangements for their care have to take this into account. Doing so will require further changes to the social work task in this arena and is likely to build on the multi-professional arrangements already in place as part of community care provisions. Whether these are self-funded, purchased through the market or supplied as universal services remains an issue for politicians to resolve, although social workers can make an input into the ensuing debates by supporting older people in expressing their views. Supplying universal services does not mean that they should all be the same, simply that these are available and easily accessed by all in need. The actual service provided should be based on sensitive responses to individuals and their unique needs, tailoring these to accord with specifications that take account of their ethnicity, 'race', gender, disability, age, religious affiliation, cultural preferences and socio-economic status.

4

Disabled People

Human Tragedies or Disabling Societies?

Social workers are legally obliged to provide services to those entitled to receive them. Operating within the principles of eligibility, they consider those worthy of services as 'deserving' and those who are not as 'undeserving'. People may be 'deserving' and still receive stigmatizing services, however. This is because, unlike health care or education for children, which are deemed universal services available to all, social services are deemed residual or stigmatized resources used primarily by poor people or those deficient in social skills if they meet eligibility criteria about need.

Disabled people have traditionally been considered a 'deserving' group, but deemed incapable of making decisions for themselves, dependent on the goodwill of others and given patronizing and stigmatizing services. This stigma often applied to their carers as well. Jonathan Parker (2007a, 2007b) has termed this 'stigma through association'. Disabled people within the disability movement call this way of relating to them the 'medical model' of disability, which casts them as human tragedies requiring sympathetic intervention by experts who know what they need. They have replaced this approach with the 'social model of disability', to highlight how *society disables* them. The disability movement claims that our social relations disable people; seeks to create alternative services that place disabled people in charge of their destiny; and challenges mainstream provisions.

The 50 million disabled people in Europe form 10 per cent of the world's disabled population; half are women; 8.6 million live in the UK. In this chapter, I consider examples of social action undertaken by disabled people to challenge social work interventions based on the medical model of disability and their demands for services that they create and run. The 1995 Disability Discrimination Act, Centres for Independent Living and direct payments came into existence through actions taken directly by disabled people seeking control over their lives and services they want. The struggle to have their voices heard in enacting their social and human rights is a key component of disabled people's narratives about accessing services (Morris, 2006).

De-Medicalizing Disability

The medical model of disability has been central to the treatment of disabled people as dependent on the goodwill of others when accessing services and resources. It has placed 'experts', usually health professionals, in charge of their existence. These professionals have defined disabled people's concerns as problems requiring medical interventions either to 'cure' their disability or to mitigate its worst effects. This approach personalizes issues and perceives disabled people as incapacitated individuals rather than resilient people with many strengths who, if allowed to access appropriate resources, can make decisions for themselves and run their lives accordingly. The medical model pathologizes disability and ignores how incapacities of various types are socially structured as problems to be addressed by individuals rather than society. Shifting this definition and the balance of power associated with professionals in favour of disabled people lies at the heart of the disability movement's struggle to de-medicalize disability and gain acceptance for the social model instead.

The disability movement defines disability as the product of the interaction between disabled people and their social, economic and physical environments. This makes social relations critical to understanding the impact of disability on people and their relationships with others. How non-disabled people interact with disabled people is key to the specific dynamics of oppression that discriminate against, humiliate and stigmatize disabled people and so are known as disablism. Within this relationship/hierarchy, those who are able-bodied exercise power to oppress and humiliate those who are impaired.

Society's views of disability portray disabled people as suffering personal tragedies that need to be treated with medical interventions that (re)produce the medical model of disability. Social workers have accepted this model and cast disabled people as deserving, but dependent. This treatment is indicative of disablism, whereby people are viewed as incapable of making decisions and dependent on others for getting on with their lives. Interacting with disabled people on this basis creates disabling relations. Within the complex of disabling relations, different groups of people experience additional forms of oppression linked to gender, 'race', class and other social divisions. For example, disabled women are stereotyped as 'less than women' or with fewer entitlements than non-disabled women. Harilyn Russo (1988) cites how learning-disabled women are denied motherhood through forced sterilizations. Nasira Begum (1992) has criticized white feminists' failure to recognize black disabled women's specific concerns. Tom Shakespeare (1999) writes of how disabled men are made to feel 'less than men'. These characterizations have arisen because able-bodiedness as the basis of the body beautiful provides the social norms against which all people are judged.

The UK's modern disability movement began in the 1970s when disabled people refused to eat regulation suppers, be locked up in institutions, and participate in restricted after-dinner activities. Instead, they demanded their say and went to pubs in wheelchairs. The movement gathered strength during the 1970s and 1980s as disabled people organized to challenge patronizing and stigmatizing treatment by both health professionals and social workers. The Union of Physically Impaired People Against Segregation (UPIAS) was one of the first in Britain. It offered a new model for dealing with disability issues to the world. UPIAS was started by disabled British activist Paul Hunt at Le Court in 1972. At that time, disabled people lived, worked and were educated in segregated facilities. They were called demeaning names and treated as if they lacked intelligence. Organizations like People First soon followed Hunt's lead. Disabled people adopted a strong advocacy element and their theorists focused on how social structures and social relations created disability. They re-theorized their position to highlight agency amongst disabled people. Agency became evident in the actions that disabled people took for themselves as they articulated the 'social model of disability' (Oliver, 1990). This placed professional discourses of disability in the social rather than personal or medical domain.

Disabled activists sought to organize services that met their needs as they defined them. In America, this included challenging insurance companies that refused medical coverage, claiming disabled people were chronically ill or poor insurance risks and unprofitable. Centres for Independent Living (CILs) were amongst the first resources that disabled people created for themselves in the UK during the 1970s. Some social workers were involved in the formation of CILs as support workers. These social workers supported disabled people by working to their agendas and endorsing the social model of disability rather than demanding the fulfilment of the professionally determined medical one. Disabled people's demands for inclusion as equals in wider society or 'normalization' entailed mainstreaming their lives and the services they needed (Wolfenberger, 1972). The disability movement gained renewed vigour in 1981 when the United Nations declared it the Year of Disabled People. The British Council of Organizations of Disabled People (BCODP) was formed in the same year. Struggles in Britain resonated in other countries as the BCODP worked for the acceptance of the social over the medical definition of disability and to secure human rights for disabled people. Disabled activists in the UK have learnt from and been supported by disabled activists across the world and offered the same in return. Their efforts resulted in the UN adopting the Convention on the Rights of Persons with Disabilities and Optional Protocol in December 2006 (with 27 ratifications by mid-2008).

At the beginning of the movement, disabled people's desire to legitimate their concerns in the public sphere led them to talk about themselves as a single group with a homogeneous or unitary identity and similar demands. This created an oppositional division between disabled and able-bodied people to highlight their oppression as a specific group. This unitary view of their identities was later challenged within the movement by disabled women and black disabled activists, who highlighted different bases in their experiences of disability. This gave rise to differentiated notions of disability and critiques about unitary identities. Known as deconstructing identities to expose differences in experiences, this showed, amongst other matters, how disabled women were denied the right to motherhood and disabled men the right to be men. Disabled women, labelled unattractive for marriage and incapable of raising children, were pressured by health and social care professionals into sterilization or having abortions, in direct contravention of their human rights and entitlement to a family life.

For this reason, Marc Quinn's statue of Alison Lapper, a disabled artist as a pregnant disabled woman, was a powerful political statement. Its artistic merit proved controversial, but having it erected on a plinth in Trafalgar Square, next to the statue of disabled hero Lord Nelson, in September 2005 was a symbolic breakthrough in the recognition of disabled women's right to have children. How many people think of Nelson as a disabled hero? The juxtaposition between Nelson and Lapper exposes the greater value given to disabled men whose disability can be ignored if sustained by heroic acts. Disabled men in general, however, are considered 'less than men' and incapable of earning a living for their families – the mark of manhood. Becoming a father is also deemed problematic, but acceptable if a non-disabled woman cares for the man. Popular novels like *Jane Eyre* depict the invisibility of gendered social relations operating within the sphere of disability. In the novel, Jane gives up her aspirations for herself in order to serve as Rochester's 'eyes'. By acting in this way, her sacrifice for her disabled husband, who is placed on a pedestal, replays patriarchal relations, where men's needs supersede those of women, in a new site, without being considered remarkable.

Replacing the Medical Model of Disability with the Social Model of Disability

Social workers played into the medical model and depicted disabled people as 'deserving' clients who were the passive recipients of care. The enactment of these attitudes perpetrates disabling social relations on the personal, institutional and cultural levels. Personal disablism focuses on the negative beliefs and attitudes that non-disabled people hold about disabled people. These are linked to views of disability as a tragedy, seeing disabled people as lesser beings and thinking disabled people are incapable of leading normal lives. Institutional disablism is the reinforcement of these attitudes and beliefs through the normal routines of practice and policies that guide professional or institutional behaviour. It undermines disabled people's claims to a good quality of life as they define it, considers them incapable of making their own decisions, and treats them as dependent on professional expertise and goodwill. Cultural disablism reflects the social values and norms that exclude disabled people from equal treatment in public arenas. Cultural disablism promotes the celebration of able-bodiedness and youthful vigour over impairment and sets up a binary division that equates able bodies with power and privilege and disabled bodies with what is provided through the generosity of others. The former constitutes the norms against which the latter is judged and found inadequate. These three dimensions of disabling relations feed into and out of each other.

Institutional disablism is of specific concern in the social care arena of social work because disabled people process requests for services through social work institutions. These become sites where abuses of power occur at their expense. Successive British governments have sought to improve institutional practice and personal functioning through performance indicators that cover equality. Managers and inspectors use these to measure how well individuals and organizations deliver services. They award 'star' ratings with financial inducements attached to motivate them into meeting performance targets, government standards and equal opportunities legislation.

These measures have not prevented abuse. A joint Healthcare Commission and Commission for Social Care Inspection Report (2006) exposed widespread institutional abuse being perpetrated upon learning-disabled people at Budock Hospital in an NHS Trust in Cornwall and recommended closure. Their investigation found that the multi-disciplinary team responsible for the care of learning-disabled people engaged in various practices that ignored guidelines in *Valuing People* (DH, 2001b). These included: the over-use of medication to control behaviour; lack of stimulation for long portions of the day; and professionals' failure to engage learning-disabled people in formulating individual care plans. The Strategic Health Authority for the area was charged with bringing practice into line with government standards.

The perpetration of unprofessional practices under the medical model of relating to learning-disabled people indicates the limited progress made in guaranteeing equality to disabled people. The exposure of such practices by an inspection indicates that the mechanisms to safeguard the rights of people accessing social services and health care can be effective. This situation demonstrates how important it is for disabled people to continue being vigilant in the services they are given and to reiterate and reinforce demands for equality. The struggle is not yet over, but social workers can support it. Disability organizations challenge social workers by identifying their disabling practices and demanding that they change their interventions to support disabled people's struggles for self-realization, life under their own control and community-based services. These moves towards independence include undertaking their own research rather than having others foist it upon them. In keeping with these developments, Michael Oliver (1990) has posited that social workers cannot empower people, only desist from disempowering them.

Alongside disabled people's struggles over service provisions and legislation are parallel conflicts over policies to recognize their human rights and demands for social justice. These have covered: recruitment for jobs and college places; health conditions for workers in social work and nursing; enlarging the definition of disability to include users of mental health services; and removing the requirement for medical recognition of mental ill health before it counts as a disability. Disabled people have fought to get discrimination on the basis of disability declared unlawful. Disability discrimination legislation and direct payments were on the list of demands to facilitate purchase of their own services and control over the care they received and who provided it. After protracted struggles, the Disability Discrimination Act 1995 and Community Care (Direct Payments) Act 1996 reflected the fruits of their labour in Britain. Direct payments (DP)s are financial resources that enable individual disabled users to exercise greater choice in accessing services. They empower disabled people to purchase their own care, enable them to choose personal assistants/carers, give them more control over service delivery and allow them to remain in their own homes. DP levels could be higher, and the activities covered could be extended to give greater flexibility in their deployment. Individual budgets, now being trialled, aim to do this.

When the Disability Discrimination Act 1995 (DDA) was enacted, a Disability Rights Commission (DRC) was set up to enforce its provisions. The DDA outlawed the treatment of disabled people 'less favourably' than others. It did not cover transport, however, and was of little assistance in redressing cases of unequal treatment. The DDA was weak and the DRC had fewer powers of enforcement than either the Commission on Race Equality (CRE) or the Equal Opportunities Commission (EOC) had in relation to 'race' and gender, respectively, and fell short of disabled people's aspirations. They demanded changes to give the DDA legislation enforcement powers equal to those covering other 'isms' like sexism and racism. Pressure on government from disabled people and criticisms from the DRC in support of their claims for equal treatment produced amendments reflected in the Disability Discrimination Act 2005. The future will reveal the capacity of the 2006 Equalities Act with the Commission for Equality and Human Rights (CEHR) to impact upon this picture. The CEHR replaced the DRC from 2007 and has to address disabled people's concerns about institutional and personal oppression.

That the Equalities Act and CEHR have to maintain and extend the strengths of their predecessors with respect to 'race', gender and disability complicates the picture. The CEHR structure provides holistic interventions that cover a range of social divisions like age, 'race', gender, disability, sexual orientation and religion, and the same powers of enforcement whatever the cause of discrimination. This structure seems problematic and there are misgivings on all counts. The Equalities legislation may be an opportunity lost if the CEHR is unable to deal with the range and complexities of intersecting forms of oppression and discrimination. Its focus on the more limited goal of discrimination may leave oppression untouched; and key bases of discrimination and oppression like class have been ignored.

Disabled people continue to be discriminated against in employment and accessing public buildings, despite the legislation. At times, creative interpretations of existing laws have bypassed legal provisions. Health and safety considerations have been amongst these. For example, *The Guardian* of 4 April 2003 reported that a 10-year-old wheelchair user was denied a ticket to a film on the grounds that fire safety could be compromised if she went into the cinema. In 2004, Easyjet refused to fly 11 friends because they were hearing-impaired and the pilot judged them a danger to the safety of other passengers and themselves in an emergency (*The Daily Mirror*, 17 January 2004). Colleges and nursing homes have used the lack of appropriate lifts into buildings to exclude disabled people for health and safety reasons, e.g., Anthony Ford-Shubrook, a 17-year-old wheelchair user, who in 2003 was refused a place at St Dominic's College, Harrow, on health and safety grounds because the computer suite was on the first floor and not easily accessible to him (BBC News, 2003b). Housing providers have threatened to evict disabled people as 'nuisances' for making noise that bothers neighbours (DRC, 2004). Carers in care homes have refused to lift disabled men and women onto hoists for being 'too heavy to lift' and a health and safety risk. In one example, the DRC went to the High Court to compel East Sussex County Council to change a blanket policy on lifting. This action followed a judicial review that disabled people asked for to challenge the 'no lifting' policy that East Sussex County Council applied in all circumstances in all facilities regardless of what happened to the person who needed help. This included being left to lie in faeces or crawl on the floor to get to a hoist while care workers who refused manually to lift disabled women looked on. The judge ruled that manual lifting is warranted to maintain a disabled person's dignity and required the local authority to remove its blanket policy. This was replaced by one that clearly specified the circumstances when no lifting was allowed, namely when the safety of the worker was at risk. However, the policy is implemented on a case-by-case basis. Nonetheless, this example illustrates how the Human Rights Act passed in Britain in 1998 has been used to promote equality for disabled people.

Disabled people have argued for change that actively promotes disability equality instead of having to prove discrimination and then tackling violations of the DDA. This distinction symbolizes a crucial difference between DDA provisions and disabled people's aspirations. Limiting the duty actively to promote equality to the public sector is a major failing in these regulations. Equality regulations that apply only to the public sector are problematic because they produce inequalities across sectors, as has already occurred in the care of older people. In this instance, they foster the exclusion of private sector homes from the European Human Rights (EHR) Act but not public sector ones. This gives differentiated access to human rights and disadvantages older people living in private establishments compared to those in public homes because a firm's concern to maintain profit margins over-rides older people's needs for care.

European legislation can promote the interests of disabled people in the UK. The Council of Europe passed a resolution on equal opportunities for disabled people on 20 December 1996: Council Directive 2000/78/EC prohibiting discrimination included disability. The Treaty of Amsterdam of 2 October 1997 covered disabled people. The British government enacted the Equalities Act with the Equalities Commission (CEHR) in 2007 to bring all forms of discrimination – 'race' and racism, sexism and disablism – under one umbrella. This was in response to European legislation requiring equality legislation in all member states. Internationally, the United Nations Convention on the Rights of Persons with Disabilities (CRPD) was adopted on 13 December 2006 by the General Assembly after years of lobbying by disabled people. This can be deployed to enforce disabled people's right to an equal place in society.

The case study below exemplifies how everyday life practices are sources of constant struggle and how the judicial system can be used to promote equality for disabled people. In it, different social divisions interact with each other to produce ethical dilemmas that can be resolved legally. The setting is Canada, but the insights it gives can be transferred to other countries that emphasize equality between different groups, e.g., the UK.

Case study: Disabled people's struggle for equality in everyday life routines

Bruce Gilmour from Vancouver, Canada, had been visually impaired for over 30 years. In November 2006, after a day's skiing, he called a taxi from a coffee shop to take him and his guide dog home. The taxi that was sent to him was driven by a practising Muslim who refused to take him because he could not associate with dogs as his religion considers them impure. Bruce deemed this treatment humiliating and a form of discrimination, albeit one that had occurred regularly in the past. This time he filed a human rights complaint against the driver and taxi firm. In August 2007, a few days before a full hearing in a Human Rights Tribunal, the taxi company signed an agreement issued by the Tribunal. This sought to balance the rights of visually impaired people with those of a Muslim cab driver to follow his religious beliefs.

The agreement required the taxi company to establish a policy that forbids any taxi driver to refuse to take any visually impaired person and certified guide dog as passengers unless he is allergic to dogs or has honest religious beliefs that prevent the transportation of certified guide dogs. In either of these instances, the driver is required to call for another taxi to be dispatched and wait with the passenger until the other cab arrives. The penalty for the first time a taxi driver violates this new company policy is a suspension that lasts for two shifts. Their contract will be terminated for a second offence. To maintain the dignity of the disabled person, he or she is not required to tell the company of impairments when calling for a taxi. (Sinoski, 2007)

This case reveals that ordinary activities become sites of struggle when different principles conflict with each other. This ensuing agreement found a way of respecting the dignity of disabled people and the right of Muslims to observe their religious beliefs. This policy is not binding on other taxi firms, but provides a model that can be used to serve visually impaired people. It exemplifies how ethical dilemmas where the rights of disabled people seemingly conflict with rights of others can, if well handled, lead to win-win situations that social workers in the UK can learn from.

Deconstructing Identities and Gendering Disability

Disability may be visible or non-visible. Susan Wendell (1996) in *The Rejected Body* describes how difficult her life was as a disabled lecturer with a non-visible disability (a viral infection). She felt people could only understand what was happening to her if they saw visible evidence of her disabled status. People's inability to see her as a disabled person to an extent parallels the invisibility of children who have been sexually abused. People may be suffering from some traumatic violation of their sense of self. If without physical bruises, they feel disempowered and unable to discuss how they are treated. Other people's reactions emphasize denial rather than empathy, understanding or non-stigmatizing support. Abolishing stereotypes of disability and dehumanizing or shaming responses are important steps in eradicating oppression and discrimination against disabled people. Another one is treating them with dignity and equality.

Disability interacts with other social divisions, e.g., 'race', gender, age, class, sexual orientation and mental ill health, to complicate the experience of disability according to those facets that apply. These should not be seen as simply additive, but as intersecting and interacting with one another to differentiate the experience of one individual from others because there are unique features that apply. Individuals have aspects of their life that they share with others like them. Theories that enable us to explain individual differences are hard to apply within a collective context, and vice versa. Collectively based theories are often unable to address individual needs. Some theories are culturally bound and cannot be assumed to be universally relevant. This is exemplified by white European male-orientated Freudian theories used in psycho-therapies (Maquire and Dewing, 2007) that transfer badly to other locations and cultures, e.g., indigenous culture in Australia or Canada or Hindu culture in India.

Disabled people can be abused by being identified as having specific expertise on disability simply because they are disabled. This presupposes a unitary identity for disabled people, negated by their actual lives. It also indicates how disability defines a person to the detriment of other aspects of their identity and skills. This was the case for Manjit in the case below, where disablist attitudes led to institutionalized abuse.

Case study: Institutional abuse of a disabled British Asian woman social worker

Manjit was a disabled woman of Sikh Asian descent who spoke Hindi, Punjabi and Urdu. She was employed as a social worker with major responsibility for working with children and families. Manjit was subjected to 'organizational creep'. This is an unrecognized increase in workload brought about by being given duties not in her job description. Colleagues assumed that Manjit could work with all black families; would be available to translate for all those who spoke Hindi, Punjabi and Urdu; and could act as the expert on disability for all people, black and white. This added substantially to her workload, which had not been reduced to take account of the increased work coming her way.

She resented this treatment because it was a misuse of her talents and time. She understood it was not ill intended, that her colleagues were trying to provide better services for service users in a context in which the office had no other black workers, it lacked translators and interpreters, and the disability team was located several miles away. This simply increased her frustration. She found it harder to address the problem as she did not like letting people down. Finally, she reached a point when she decided it should not be seen as a personal issue between her and her colleagues. She decided to address the fundamental problem of the inadequate resourcing of the office at a team meeting so that they could plan how to raise her concerns with management. Her colleagues were initially surprised at the suggestion that she was being misused and unfairly treated.

Manjit explained her point of view, saying simply that as a multi-lingual disabled black woman, she was not an expert in all the areas she has been asked to address, and that she had to work harder to find time to do the work that she had been employed to do because so much more was expected of her. Once this message sank in, the entire team settled down to work out how to present a collective case to senior management for appropriate resourcing of the office.

Manjit's situation is one that would resonate amongst disabled black men and women, who are often asked to undertake tasks not in their job descriptions to compensate for institutional failings. Manjit's solution places responsibility for changing the situation squarely on the local authority, where it belongs. It also demonstrates how structural deficiencies have serious implications for individuals. Elsewhere (Dominelli, 1988), I have identified as a form of institutional abuse the inadequate resourcing of social services in a multicultural society that proclaims to address diversity in the expectation that workers will deal with resource shortages. It exploits a person's humanity and wish to help others, but leaves structural issues untouched. Tackling these could involve working across different professional groupings, advocating for change and lobbying politicians and other resource-holders.

Disabled people have worked in inter-disciplinary teams involving health and social services. Inter-disciplinary teams may be referred to as partnerships, multi-disciplinary teams or inter-agency teams. During the 1980s, innovative examples of such working involved disabled people as full participants in determining policies and practice and gave rise to Independent Living initiatives. Inter-disciplinarity across the health–social care interface has been further promoted by the Health Act 1999. Patient Advice and Liaison Services (PALS) currently support people who seek access to health and social services facilities. These schemes engage disabled people in broad inter-disciplinary social networks that build effective interpersonal relationships to deliver services to those living independently at home. Social workers facilitate these networks by forming and coordinating links and liaising between people and agencies and across agencies to ensure that specified work is carried out.

There is also a representational component: each professional in the team represents his or her employing agency. Inter-agency work transfers knowledge across agencies, encourages participation amongst all those involved in planning, and makes decisions about and evaluates particular interventions. This should include service users wherever possible (Warren, 2007). Participants consult those with an interest in what is happening but who might not be directly involved in an activity. Professionals reach out to others within their own specialist areas of knowledge. Tensions and conflict can arise between different professional groups as they hold different priorities, have different cultural traditions, and interpret situations in ways consistent with expertise and values. Understanding how various systems operate and interact with each other is crucial to working effectively across professional boundaries if delivering services that utilize contributions from diverse organizations. For these reasons, social workers acquire coordination and liaison roles.

The case study below indicates the complexities of working with disabled people who have multiple needs in old age and limited social networks to support them. It also exposes the strengths and weaknesses of multi-agency working in such situations.

Case study: The limitations of community care in meeting the complex needs of older disabled people

Gladys lived alone. She suffered a serious stroke just after her 74th birthday and required hospitalization. This exacerbated her paralysis and forgetfulness. She had made good physical progress with physiotherapy and was keen to return to her own home. A psychogeriatrician undertook various tests, including a Mini-Mental State Examination (MMSE) to assess her cognitive functions. These revealed some cognitive impairment, but nothing serious enough for him to suggest residential care. The social worker felt that Gladys was not ready to return home at this point, but the hospital insisted, and to avoid paying a penalty for a delayed discharge, she agreed to make the necessary arrangements. At Gladys's request, this included asking a neighbour, Ben, to keep an eye on her and let her know if Gladys's condition deteriorated. Ben agreed to help out.

Gladys's post-discharge plan allowed her to remain at home with support from her GP of many years and a care manager/social worker who would be responsible for organizing and monitoring a package of care for her and coordinating activities with the other professionals involved, especially those in the health sector. The care manager arranged for domiciliary care and an agency to help Gladys clean the house. Care agency workers came each evening to get Gladys into bed. The care manager arranged for Gladys to attend a day centre three mornings a week and monitored her progress by visiting or phoning regularly.

Gladys was confused about why there were so many people in her life, but the first few weeks of her return home passed by uneventfully. However, the care staff grew increasingly worried about her failure to sleep adequately in the evenings, despite the mild sedative prescribed by her GP. About six weeks after her discharge, the police found Gladys wandering in a nearby park after midnight with only night clothes on. She was looking for her dead husband and appeared unaware of where she was. The police called the out-of-hours duty team, who got her admitted to the psychiatric wing of a hospital some distance away because there were no residential places or psychiatric services in the immediate locality. The primary health trust had closed these when local services were centralized to reduce expenditures. When she found herself in a psychiatric ward with more seriously disturbed people, Gladys became more distressed. She cried that she wanted to go home. She had never considered herself as having mental health problems, just forgetfulness, and was sure that she could manage at home if Ben continued to help her. But the social worker decided that she had only one option: to plan long-term residential care for Gladys.

Gladys's situation exemplifies care that aspires to meet an older person's needs, but fails to do so within a framework of human rights and citizenship. Facilities have not been developed to respond to the needs of older people, particularly those with a complex range of needs. In Gladys's case, from the information available, these are likely to include issues around disability, poor health, problematic mental health, social isolation, poverty and possibly grief over the loss of her husband/companion. A social worker could help her address these. The absence of facilities to do so can be considered an infringement of older people's human rights and dignity, but this stance would require a court case to prove it. Today's older people grew up under scarcity conditions engendered by World War II, are reluctant to complain about their treatment, and tend to either accept the services proffered or reject them and insist that they remain in their own homes, as Gladys did.

The social workers, health professionals and care workers had other options that they might have considered for Gladys if they had intervened earlier in a preventative capacity. They could have engaged her in discussions about how to meet her needs (including grieving for her husband), improve her social networks and involve her more in leisure activities with other people to reduce her isolation and improve a poor quality of life. Given time, social workers could build a relationship based on trust that would enable Gladys to grow in her willingness to interact with others and acquire confidence in doing so.

Conclusions

Disabled people have been considered a 'deserving' category of service users. This has not excluded them from being deprived of the right to make their own decisions. Nor does it prevent them from receiving stigmatized services that do not always meet their needs. Professional interventions based on a medical model of disability promote the view that disability is a personal tragedy best treated with medical interventions by professional experts who know best what to do in the life of a given individual, not a socially created situation that disadvantages disabled people.

Disabled people highlighted the disabling nature of society and took control of their destiny to create the social model of disability, to form alternative services for their use, and to demand the same rights to equality as everyone else. These became incorporated into what became known as 'normalization'. Whilst disabled people have made gains, including the Disability Discrimination Act and direct payments, they still are not accorded the status of first-class citizens. Key areas such as equal rights to employment, access to social resources, health services and housing to meet their needs remain elusive. The institutional abuse of learning-disabled people at Budock Hospital indicates the vast gap between theory and practice to be covered in treating disabled people in an egalitarian manner. Disabled people have been viewed as a unitary group, all having one identity and set of experiences. They have challenged this construction of their situation within the disability movement itself and in wider society. They have highlighted the diversity of their movement and the importance of having services that meet their diverse needs and expectations and are placed under their control. If social workers want to promote empowerment processes, they are asked to support the autonomy of disabled people by working with them rather than treating them as passive recipients of care.

5

Mental Ill Health

Care in Institutions or the Community?

Mental illness has been defined as a stigmatizing condition. Until recent times, people labelled 'mentally ill' were left in inhumane institutions under appalling forms of treatment that violated their human rights and denied their capacity to decide matters for themselves. They were assumed incapable of behaving according to accepted social norms and associated with danger, violence or disease. Erving Goffman's (1961) brilliant analysis of institutional care in the 1960s exposed oppressive regimes of control that operated primarily to serve the interests of the institution and staff. Medication was used to control or discipline patients who disrupted institutional professional regimes rather than assist them in a return to independent life.

These attitudes fostered images that inspired fear or pity. Radical psychiatrists like R.D. Laing (1969), Thomas Szasz (1972) and Duncan Double (2005), as well as survivors of this treatment, wanted change, a return of patients' human rights and citizenship status. Despite such efforts, *Modernising Mental Health Services*, published by the Department of Health (1999), presents users of mental health services as risks posing a danger to others or themselves, not whole persons with the potential to grow.

In this chapter, I demonstrate how the stigmatizing 'mentally ill' label has a strong, and often negative, impact on the services mentally ill people can access. I also highlight the initiatives that people surviving mental ill health have undertaken to assert their rights and change their treatment. This exposes the tensions between self-determination, user-empowerment and social control. Issues of social justice and social inclusion are also relevant to the demands raised by mentally ill people. I consider these through case examples.

The Social Construction of Mental Illness

Mental ill health involves complex interactions between the biological, psychological and 'social' domains. What constitutes or is defined as mental illness is socially constructed. People define acceptable and unacceptable behaviour, labelling those deviating from acceptable norms as 'deviant' or mentally ill. Mental illness had traditionally been treated as an abnormality that people sought to stay away from, with those labelled as mentally ill placed in out-of-town asylums to protect those not so afflicted. Fear of users of mental health services is still reflected today in popular resistance to proposals to site mental health establishments or community-based provisions for those with mental health problems in residential neighbourhoods. The locating of psychiatric hospitals or clinics in these is fiercely resisted.

Meanwhile, by the 1980s, the land where residential establishments like psychiatric hospitals were once located had become extremely valuable. As part of the modernizing processes of opening up public provisions to the private sector, the public authorities that owned these lands sold them. The sale of these assets has reduced the range of facilities catering for those with mental ill health problems who cannot be cared for in the community, thereby creating difficulties for social workers seeking high-quality residential care for them. The developers who purchased these sites have made huge profits by building private luxury housing estates that those who have experienced mental ill health cannot afford, rather than investing in high-quality mental health services. Central Hospital, a psychiatric hospital in Hatton, Warwickshire, for example, opened in 1852 as a former lunatic asylum and virtually self-sufficient community set on 70 acres of woodlands. It closed in 1994 and was later sold by the local authority. In 2003, it was developed into luxury housing available for purchase.

Critiques of the inappropriate handling of mentally ill people have led to calls for the de-institutionalization of their treatment and relocation in the community. The idea is laudable in its aims to improve therapeutic responses to mental illness. However, the government's failure to fund these initiatives adequately has meant that mentally ill people have been released into communities without adequate back-up. As high-quality residential establishments needed by some are often unavailable, mentally ill people can lack adequate supervision and get into trouble when they do not take medication. This is what happened in the case of Christopher Clunis, who became a *cause célèbre* in the neglect of those dumped in communities without dependable support networks or adequate professional assistance.

In 1992, Clunis, in a random and vicious attack, killed Jonathan Zito, who was waiting for an underground train at Finsbury Park station, London, on his way home from work. This tragic murder shocked a public that had failed to connect general indifference to mentally ill people with the appalling consequences that follow society's inadequate responses to their care. Press coverage tapped into a strong public perception that associates mental health problems with danger, violence and fear and reinforced stereotypical responses and discourses emphasizing the withdrawal of the right of those using mental health services to participate in broader society.

There is an enormous task of public education to be undertaken to instruct the public in the importance of recognizing and addressing mental ill health within a framework of human rights, social justice and citizenship. This is essential in enabling the public to appreciate mental ill health as a product of a society that is socially constructed to separate 'normal' people from those labelled 'insane' and 'other'. One such public campaign was the Like Minds Campaign in New Zealand/Aotearoa (Like Minds, 2007). This emphasized similarities between users of mental health services and non-users. It revealed that the link between violence and mental ill health did not apply to most users of mental health services and that many were gainfully employed, participated in community activities and raised families. Similar campaigns in the UK could involve social workers as advocates making links between these two groups. Social workers' support of a human rights perspective in this field of practice is crucial in linking the liberty of people with mental health problems with concerns about minimizing harm to themselves and others.

The oppression of users of mental health services is called mentalism. The dynamics that underpin this form of oppression separate people who are mentally ill from those who are 'normal'. Segregating people with mental ill health problems from daily interactions with those who are not is central to 'othering' mentally ill people. 'Othering' justifies differentiated treatment that assumes inequality between various groups in society and leads to discrimination and oppression and ultimately unequal life chances between the two groups. 'Othering' is a form of social exclusion that creates one group as the in-group (us) and the other as the out-group (them), and ascribes superiority to the in-group and inferiority to the out-group. The 'them–us' construction makes it easier to stigmatize and negatively stereotype those in the out-group. Power and privileges are accorded to the in-group while the out-group is denied these. In the case of mental ill health, those not mentally ill are seen as superior, an idea that underpins the withdrawal of human rights and decision-making powers from users of mental health services. Mentalism legitimates oppressive practices in the latter's 'care' by professionals who exercise power over them.

Human Rights: An Issue for Users of Mental Health Services

The long-established tradition of locking people with mental ill health in psychiatric institutions under medical control stigmatized these people and subjected them to regimes of control that prioritized institutional and professional considerations over theirs (Goffman, 1961). Derogatory terms such as 'lunatic' depicted their low status and served as codes for those incapable of looking after themselves and dangerous to interfere with. Fear and violence combined to form powerful images of those so labelled. Institutions ostensibly catering for their needs were located out of town in green-field sites, away from the public gaze, although in small rural areas there might be a village 'idiot' who was tolerated as an object of ridicule (Malin, 1995). The absence of human rights and autonomy in the 'treatment' of those who were 'mentally ill' has had profound implications for contemporary attitudes towards those given this label.

One in four of the population is expected to experience a mental health problem. About 250,000 people in the UK receive psychiatric services at any one time. Some groups in the population may be more vulnerable than others so labelled: women have a greater propensity for depression; 40 per cent of young people experience periods of mental distress; and black and minority ethnic groups are disproportionately labelled 'mentally ill' (Littlewood and Lipsedge, 1997). Nevertheless, mental ill health can affect anyone at any point in life. Renowned politicians have experienced mental health problems, e.g., Winston Churchill, a point highlighted by the mental health charity Rethink in 2006 when it commissioned a controversial sculpture of him wearing a straitjacket

(BBC News, 2006). The example of Churchill shows that mental ill health does not necessarily incapacitate a person from having a productive life. The dividing line between a person who has a mental health problem and one who does not can be blurred and messy.

Users of mental health services are employed below their level of qualifications in poorly paid, low-status jobs like street-sweepers and farm workers. Many find that, having acquired this label, they are unlikely to be hired in any post with substantial responsibilities or extensive interactions with the public. A government survey of the only UK programme that aimed to get disabled people into the labour market revealed that 37 per cent of employers would not employ people who were or had been mentally ill, compared to 62 per cent who would hire disabled people with other impairments. Those holding senior positions, including management, prior to the onset of mental ill health faced demotion upon return to work (Batty, 2004). This response is an active form of risk management based in a benevolent paternalism that undermines people's human rights. Employers react to minimize risk to individual employees and others in case previous responsibilities offer overly stressful situations. The Disability Discrimination Act (DDA) 1995 prohibited such discrimination. Yet, users of mental health services constituted 28 per cent of those using its provisions to challenge ill-treatment by employers. They were also least likely to succeed in their claims. The persistence of these results caused the Disability Rights Commission (DRC) to ask government to strengthen the DDA for mental health users in 2003.

Critiques of the treatment of mental health service users, particularly powerful in the anti-psychiatry movement of the 1960s and 1970s, led to calls for the closure of psychiatric institutions that responded poorly to their needs. Their demands were echoed by those advocating community care provisions during the 1980s and 1990s and became part of the 'de-institutionalization' movement. This emphasized the care of people experiencing mental ill health in the community under circumstances that involved mental health service users in decisions about them. The lack of resources for community care and highly publicized cases of people being killed by mentally ill individuals, however, logged the initiative a failure in public consciousness and highlighted communities' inability to respond adequately to mental health service users.

Mental health issues are interesting and complex because they bring together not only inter-agency working but also interactions among the biological, psychological and social aspects of human life. Social workers have to work with all these dimensions when practising a holistic approach to mental ill health. Statistics that differentiate amongst various factors help to determine how different groups of people experience mental ill health and how they are treated by mental health practitioners. Issues of class, gender, 'race' and age are important indicators of how people are treated by mental health experts. Those responding within a mentalist framework associate mental ill health with a deficit or disability that has to be made good. Conventional mental health practitioners respond to difference by medicalizing patients' conditions and denying services that deliver their human rights and enhance their capacities for engaging with others as whole human beings. In unpacking the significance of 'race' and gender in mental ill health outcomes, research has revealed connections between the social construction of people's place and status in society and responses to them. These often legitimate exclusion from public life and loss of human rights while being treated by experts in 'psy' professions like psychology or psychiatry (Nazroo, 1999).

'Othering' occurs in several dimensions because mental ill health intersects and interacts with 'race', gender and other social divisions to differentiate a group's experiences of mental ill health from the white heterosexual European male 'norm'. Challenges to the medical model in professional responses to mental ill health began in the 1970s when individual pathology as the explanation for these difficulties was suffused with understandings about the social construction of mental ill health.

George Brown and Tirril Harris (1978) showed that women are more likely to suffer depression as a result of social demands upon them as women, namely being responsible for the care and nurture of others. In the 1970s, women working with women in community settings rejected the tranquillizers GPs prescribed to enable them to cope with these demands. They criticized this response for individualizing their situation and preventing them from questioning their status. Feminist social action in the field of mental ill health initiated alternative responses that highlighted the significance of child care and mental health services that women designed and ran (Kornstein and Clayton, 2002). Young adolescent women are deemed mentally ill if they have eating disorders, despite challenges to these conditions' medicalization by feminist social workers, who linked them to the social position of young women (McLeod, 1982). Suman Fernando's (1991) analyses of mental health services indicated that black people, especially young men of Afro-Caribbean origins, were sectioned involuntarily and considered schizophrenic. This picture still applies today (Bhopal, 1998; Fernando, 2001). Cultural differences become strong predictors of mental illness as the police, medical practitioners, psychiatrists and social workers misinterpret behaviour they are unfamiliar with as 'dangerous' and likely to harm the person concerned or others. 'Race', gender and other social divisions cannot be ignored without losing the potential to respond appropriately to mental health users.

Questioning the Expertise of the 'Psy' Professions

Social workers play key roles in: empowering users of mental health services; safeguarding human rights; applying for admission to hospital for compulsory psychiatric care (with or without the support of a near relative); preventing abuse by other professionals and individuals; monitoring and reviewing care plans following discharge; conducting risk assessments on service users; and compiling social circumstances reports for mental health review tribunals. Mental health services in the UK today are accessed through Community Mental Health Trusts with or without outreach activities in community-based multi-professional teams composed of medical practitioners, nurses and social workers without medical training (Golightley, 2006). In the hierarchy of groups constituting the 'psy' professions, as those with expertise in mental health are called, social workers occupy the lowest rung. At the top are psychiatrists and psychologists. Their methods of working, including the medical model, are paramount. The valuing of medical professional expertise in the daily routines of users of mental health services skews social workers' interventions away from the sphere of the 'social', which focuses on interpersonal relationships or how people interact with each other, in favour of the medical dimension.

Until the 1983 Mental Health Act was revised in 2007, social workers had to be local authority employees and receive additional training as Approved Social Workers (ASWs) to practise in mental health. ASW training occurred after qualifying training or basic qualifications had been obtained and was required prior to practice. This made working with mental health service users a specialism beyond the scope of a qualified social worker with generic training. The 2007 Mental Health Act replaced the ASW with the Approved Mental Health Practitioner (AMHP). The AMHP is appointed by a local authority and can hold any qualification, including a social work one. Although AMHPs should understand the social model of mental distress, only the ASW holds training that is rooted in the social sciences and has a perspective independent of a medical practitioner. It is too early to pronounce on the impact of the AMHP in removing mental health work from the remit of specialized social workers. It is presented as an initiative that deals with the lack of recruitment and retention in the ASW role. It seems a retrograde step as it does not link AMHP status or training with any specific degree programme, let alone social work. Even in social work, post-qualifying training in mental health, which an AMHP with a social work background might take, is not so linked. Nor is there a requirement to take research methods and ensure that cutting-edge knowledge is acquired by AMHPs. This approach, endorsed by the General Social Care Council in 2006, is unlikely to assist the process of deeper professionalization in this area of practice, raise its status or assure users of mental health services concerned about losing the independence symbolized by an ASW.

Medical models treat mental health service users as cogs in medical interventions and isolate them from others. People can resist this treatment, as Gloria does below.

Case study: Mothering under stressful conditions

Gloria, a single-parent mother of Afro-Caribbean descent from Birmingham, lived on benefits with five children aged from 10 years to 1 in a two-bedroom terrace in a poor housing estate in southern England. She felt extremely lucky to have been housed, after a long struggle, in any kind of social housing that was deemed acceptable by the local authority. Her original application for a four-bedroom house had been refused for being from outside the area. She was now on a waiting list for it. The estate, meanwhile, had few public amenities and taking a bus to town was expensive. Gloria managed by 'making do' and denying herself food, clothing, recreational pursuits and luxuries to meet the children's needs. Neglecting her own needs made her very run-down.

The estate had no one else of Afro-Caribbean descent living on it. Gloria knew her immediate neighbours of white English descent, but did not socialize with them. A key reason for this, other than lack of money, was that Gloria remained in the house looking after her children most of the time with limited help from the children's three fathers. She also felt uncomfortable around her neighbours, whose negative attitudes towards her and her children conveyed the message that she did not belong there and intensified her consciousness of the racialized tensions between them. The isolation and hopelessness of her situation drove Gloria to the depths of despair, but she could see no way out.

Gloria worked hard to send the three children who were old enough to nearby schools, but worried that their standards were too low for them to escape the ghetto of poverty she felt trapped by. She took her youngest two children to 'Sure Start', a community-based programme that New Labour created to help the children of poor parents have a reasonable chance of succeeding in school. Gloria thought that 'Sure Start' was a good idea, but insufficient. She also felt that no one was interested in her own specific needs because her children were not truanting or otherwise getting into trouble. She was seen as a good mother who wanted the best for her children and 'looked promising' as a parent who would keep the children out of trouble and make limited demands on the state.

Just before the Easter break, Gloria's eldest child, Belinda, woke to the sound of her mother crying inconsolably. She went to her bedroom and asked what was wrong. Gloria only cried harder and harder. She refused to get up or talk to her daughter, even though Belinda pointed out that she needed help to get ready for school. Belinda did not know what to do, but felt she should get her brother and sister to school. They got dressed and had a few flakes of cereal for breakfast before telling their mother they were leaving for school. Gloria did not reply, but continued crying. Belinda tried hard to focus on her lessons, but worrying about her mother made it difficult to concentrate on what was being said.

Her teacher noted this unusual behaviour. Belinda was an active pupil, amongst the most conscientious and brightest in the class. She was concerned, but not sure what to do. During the morning break, she spoke to Belinda's brother's teacher in the playground. She intensified her fears by saying he was also acting out of character. He had been aggressive at the beginning of class and stared out of the window most of the morning. They decided to ask the social worker in education welfare to see Belinda. The social worker saw Belinda during the lunch-break and got her to talk of her concerns about her mother. There had been other occasions when the mother's behaviour had worried the little girl, but she said there had been no one that she felt she could turn to. The social worker asked Belinda to work hard on her studies and not worry about her mother too much because she would see her immediately to offer help. A relieved Belinda went back to class and paid more attention to the lessons.

The social worker visited Gloria at home and found her still in bed crying. The two youngest children were with her on the bed, also crying. It was clear that neither had been washed or fed since the previous night. The social worker got little cooperation from Gloria and became very concerned about the children's welfare. She thought that Gloria was clinically depressed and called an ASW to join her. The ASW thought that the diagnosis of depression was probable, but needed medical verification. They both spoke to Gloria about her situation and suggested that she should seek medical attention from her GP and/or a psychiatrist who could help address her depression. As Gloria had no immediate sources of help available, they thought that the children could be (voluntarily) accommodated with foster parents to give her a break from the stress of looking after them. They advised Gloria that as there were no families of Afro-Caribbean descent on their lists, the children would be placed with a white family of English descent who had no knowledge of Afro-Caribbean culture or links with black communities. They offered to keep them together.

Gloria said 'no'. She did not want this as her mother or sister in Birmingham would look after the children if someone could ask them. She wanted pills to reduce depression and assist in caring for them at home. The social workers thought this feasible, checked it out and planned to intervene on this basis.

If the social workers involved in this case thought that Gloria was seriously ill or a danger to the children, they could have sought a compulsory admission under the 1983 Mental Health Act. Section 12 allows for the compulsory admission of someone with mental health problems into a psychiatric institution provided that two medical opinions confirm the diagnosis. An approved social work practitioner can confirm this response under Section 12(2). The social workers working with Gloria did not invoke this provision because they deemed that with the appropriate safeguards in place, the risk posed to the children could be managed effectively. With medication, Gloria was unlikely to harm herself or others. The social workers were prepared to revise their assessment should circumstances change or kin care (care by relatives) prove unavailable. As they acted with these understandings, they were able to limit their potential 'to do to' Gloria and 'do with' her. In this sense, social workers, whether ASWs or not, can choose how to use power and authority. This choice can make the difference between leaving service users feeling that they have been listened to or thinking they have been oppressed by the help that was to enable them cope more effectively with their situations and facilitate their taking control of their lives. Empowering support for users of mental health services involves a partnership where professionals listen closely to and work with users to agree a plan of action, not impose services on them.

Gloria's situation reflects the inadequate provisions available for poor mothers with children to help in the important task of raising them. These include the absence of decent round-the-clock child care facilities and readily accessible, flexible respite care for parents with domestic responsibilities. These could prevent crises like this one from arising. While social workers initially took charge of Gloria's situation and made plans without her involvement because she would not cooperate, they responded quickly to revise their views when she made alternative suggestions that took account of their concerns about the safety of the children. Not labelling her as 'sick', but as in need of assistance to control her life helped them treat Gloria with respect and dignity and as a person with the capacity to make decisions that would benefit both her and the children. This affirms her human rights rather than detracting from them.

For Gloria to progress beyond the immediate crisis, the social workers would have to work with her to extend her social networks. This would have been a significant challenge given that other people of Afro-Caribbean descent did not live locally. Access to black communities was needed to enable the children to develop relationships with black adults and children. Advocacy work to address Gloria's housing, employment, educational and recreational needs and link her up with black communities would have been central to this case. Inter-agency communication and longer-term, effective working with other professionals in the medical, psychiatric, psychological, social services, education and voluntary sectors were also essential.

Gloria's crisis was also a response to the structural limitations she endured – poor, overcrowded housing; lack of adequate child care resources or respite care; the absence of foster parents able to respond to the children's cultural needs; poverty and inadequate income levels; isolation; and lack of social networks or other forms of social capital. Although sensitive to her plight, the social workers were unable to deal with the structural limitations that placed Gloria in this position. Their prime concern in this situation was the children and not Gloria *per se*.

Feminist social workers would have sought ways of combining the two. Women like Gloria have to 'look after themselves' as human beings with needs outside their child care responsibilities. Receiving help to meet these is a reasonable expectation in a society believing that we each should realize our potential and become involved in and contribute to the wider society. Failure to provide resources for women implicates society in producing mental ill health as they struggle to cope with heavy responsibilities in unremitting conditions of oppression and isolation. This problem is as socially constructed as is labelling those who are mentally ill 'dangerous' people and to be avoided.

New Labour's modernization programme seeks to improve mental health services, affirming the role of choice, quality of life considerations and addressing social exclusion. *Modernising Mental Health Services* (DH, 1999) and the Care Programme Approach (CPA) outlined by the Department of Health (DH, 1990) and the 2007 Mental Health Act were central to its commitment. The CPA involves multi-disciplinary team-working with mental health service users in drawing up and reviewing a care plan. It provides a holistic and seamless service with a key worker or care coordinator to engage and support the service user in the community and link up with other professionals. Encouraging lone mothers to enter waged work can be part of this plan. They are often interested in part-time waged working that fits around their 'motherwork'. If given adequate training and child care support, they can successfully achieve this balance.

Assessment of Mental Ill Health and Risk Management

Professional intervention in cases of mental ill health in the UK involved making assessments under the 1983 Mental Health Act (MHA) until recently. The 2007 Mental Health Act replacing it empowers mental health service users in a way the 1983 MHA did not. The passage of the 2007 legislation was protracted and controversial. Mental health activists campaigned through organizations like the National Association for Mental Health (MIND) for legislation that allowed those capable of making their own decisions to do so. Sympathetic mental health practitioners supported their claims. Disagreements over what empowering users of mental health services meant led the House of Commons to reject the Bill proposing this. However, service user involvement was upheld in *Our Health, Our Care, Our Say: A New Direction for Community Services* (DH, 2006).

Assessments involve calculations of risk. For people with mental ill health these focus on their potential to harm themselves or others. Risk assessment and risk management involve processes of assessment, planning, monitoring and review. These seek to: identify hazards in the person and his or her biopsychosocial environment; assess the extent to which these are dangerous to the self and others; and predict the likelihood of harm actually taking place. A risk assessment highlights tasks to be undertaken by both service user and practitioner. Risk assessments are used to manage behaviour and reduce the chances of harm occurring. This is known as risk minimization. Actual performance against predicted outcomes is constantly monitored and reviewed to adjust the risk assessment plan as required. Vernon Quinsey (1995) claims that risk assessments are not scientific instruments and should not be treated as such, despite temptations to do so, because their capacity to predict actual behaviour in specific circumstances is extremely limited. They are better viewed as tools that enable mental health practitioners to make informed judgements and form holistic critical reflective understandings of the complexities in specific situations. The ideal is to provide proactive responses that engage service users in what has to be done, but this is tricky to maintain, and often people experience feelings of alienation and disenchantment with the process.

Risk assessments are seen as one-off interventions in a care plan, when they should be undertaken as a constant process of engagement between social worker and service user. This is rarely achieved in practice because it requires costly and intensive involvement from professionals who have limited scope in forming the helping relationships known as relational social work. Pressured social workers are more likely to use checklist-based risk assessments favoured under risk management protocols. These aim to speed up the assessment process. They reduce the possibility of resources being used for subsidiary purposes that might bring long-term benefits that are not measurable or quantifiable over the short term. An example of this might be noting the likelihood of actually taking medicine as instructed without focusing on those aspects of a person's life that enable them to enjoy relationships with others, e.g., having a hobby that enables them to relate to members of their local community.

Checklist-based assessments can jeopardize the human rights and citizenship basis of people who are labelled mentally ill. For example, Philip Johnston in the *Daily Telegraph* of 10 December 2003 claimed that 400 mentally ill people were living in hostels close to Victoria Park in the London district of Hackney, where a woman jogger had been murdered.

No one had been arrested for this crime and no one knew who had murdered the woman at the time. Johnston's response symbolizes the ease with which mental health service users are labelled risks, 'dangerous' to the wider community and denied their human rights. It reveals that a presumption of innocence until proven guilty does not apply to users of mental health services. And it signifies movement towards a 'risk-averse' society, where practitioners are expected to eliminate risk rather than simply reduce it. This goal is impossible as risk assessments are not sufficiently developed to realize this aim.

Practitioners work together across a range of professions in multidisciplinary teams to provide mental health services. The idea behind such collaborations is that service users can be empowered to assume responsibility for their mental health and develop effective coping strategies and resilient attitudes towards the environment. These interventions minimize the risk of relapse and harm. Risk assessments can be undertaken by a collective inter-disciplinary team endeavour rather than the efforts of an isolated worker. This enables tasks and information to be shared more readily across a team of people. Inter-disciplinary teamworking is not as effective in practice as it should be, however. Inquiries into situations involving users of mental health services have exposed poor communication links between different professional groups. This mirrors difficulties experienced by child protection professionals. Another problem is the absence of clear definitions of roles and responsibilities for each professional involved in the care plan that is developed for a specific user.

Innovative Responses to Mental Ill Health

Mental health practitioners and politicians instanced an imaginative and novel response to mentally ill people in Bologna, Italy, in the 1980s. Developed in this city when it was under Communist Party control, these became known as the 'Red Bologna' Initiatives and promoted the re-integration of mentally ill people in the community (Jaggi et al., 1977). Facilities focused on group living accompanied by professional and lay support for small groups of users of mental health services based in a house or apartment like that of any other person. They were supported by local people and practitioners skilled in ensuring they took medication as required. More importantly, these mental health service users were assisted to hold down jobs, undertake education to (re)skill them in new occupations, and develop a circle of friends who engaged them socially and reduced social isolation and stigma.

The 'Red Bologna' Initiatives acquired world-wide fame and provided a model of user empowerment emulated in other countries (Berardi et al., 1999). Some of its principles were studied by British psychiatrists and academics and adapted for use in the UK. These initiatives were undermined, however, when the Communist Party lost local authority control to the Christian Democrats. This is a reminder that political interference in practice is an occupational hazard that social workers constantly address, regardless of the arena of practice or country in which they work. At the beginning of the twenty-first century, an Italian farmer began a new venture by introducing a monitored rehabilitation regime for mentally disordered offenders in his vineyards. He provided on-the-job training, helped them achieve their target of becoming useful members of society, and encouraged their interaction with local people. By doing so, he gave them a role in society and made them feel valued instead of ignored and locked away. In the 1970s, China used similar ideas to reintegrate mentally ill offenders into communities, asking local people to prepare them for life post-release, including their obtaining and holding down socially useful jobs (*Open Mind*, 1980).

Medical practice is relevant to working with users of mental health services, but a key difficulty is that medical experts are in charge of 'treatments'. They take little note of social factors or service users' need to control their lives. Even with safeguards, these experts take decisions that reduce service users' capacity to take charge of situations. In working with mental health service users, social workers have to know the specifics of a medical condition and drugs associated with treatment so that they can support users in leading useful and engaged lives. It is not a matter of the 'social' over the 'medical', but of the two interacting effectively to deliver the best services for a given individual in a specific social context. Social workers can also counter practices that utilize expertise to disempower service users and undermine their ability to do things for themselves. Time is required to ensure that people with mental ill health are adequately supported in staying in their own homes if they wish, and that their equal opportunities are upheld. Hence, time and relationship-building are crucial components of working with mental health service users. Both are in short supply, but social workers could stretch their resources more by working with volunteers to develop circles of lay support for use when professional expertise is not needed.

Conclusion

Encouraging dialogue and raising hope for a better future for mental health service users is a key social work task. Social workers can shift public attitudes away from denying mental health service users' human rights or entitlement to jobs for which they qualify towards seeing them as people who contribute to society. Removing the stigma associated with psychiatric disabilities will not be easy. Social workers can work with mental health service users to advocate for sensitive and well-resourced facilities that support useful lives in the community and well-resourced psychiatric settings if necessary. This will give care in the community a social justice focus and deliver a human rights- and citizenship-based model of intervention for people with mental ill health.

6

Homeless People

Independence or Social Neglect?

Homelessness is such a negative label. I much prefer to think of myself as 'rent subsidyless'.

(*Now*, 25 October 2006: 16)

Homelessness continues to be a major social problem for which there is no simple solution. In the UK, the charity Shelter began a campaign to house homeless people during the 1960s, but its goal of sufficient housing for all has yet to be met. The number of new households formed yearly outstrips that of the houses built – 213,000 to 173,000, respectively, causing the shortfall to rise annually, most heavily in social housing. The shortage in housing supply exacerbates problems caused by unaffordable housing for those on low or average incomes, and 1.5 million people are on council lists waiting to be housed. In 2007, Prime Minister Gordon Brown promised to tackle this problem by encouraging a yearly construction of 240,000 houses, including social housing in eco-villages and towns to reach a target of 3 million by 2020. Investing in high-quality social housing for homeless people could provide the subsidy they need.

Homeless people may be found in a variety of situations, ranging from living in overcrowded accommodation with relatives or friends to 'sleeping rough' on the streets. They are not accepted on local authority lists for social housing, including council housing, if kicked out by those who agreed to house them for short periods. They may be deemed to have made themselves intentionally homeless and are not entitled to housing support from the local authority. The shortage in social housing has meant that different claimants' needs are prioritized and the needs of one group in housing need may be pitted against those of another. Pregnant women, couples with children or women assaulted by partners top the lists. The Homelessness Act 2002 includes 16- to 17-year-olds and care leavers aged 18–20 as priority groups. Social workers can assist homeless families on several levels – benefit advice, housing applications, sending children to school, feeding and clothing them. Since April 2003, they have supported them in partnership with the Housing Department through the Supporting People Programme.

For other homeless adults – those who have no dependent children defined as either 'in need' or 'at risk', or who are not older people requiring community care services that involve their being housed in nursing or residential care – statutory social workers offer no support. Their exclusion becomes a way of rationing social workers' time and limited resources devoted to adults in need. Social workers working in voluntary settings support homeless people, especially teenagers, helping them to re-establish relationships with parents or other carers, find accommodation, continue their education, find jobs and acquire skills necessary for looking after themselves. They also embark on soup runs for homeless people sleeping on the streets and support homeless people with the slimmest of resources at their disposal – a lack of resources that devalues their endeavours.

In this chapter, I explore young people's stories of life on the street – the support they offer each other to survive violent and exploitative situations, especially if drawn into prostitution, drug crime and youth gangs. I identify coping strategies, resilience and vulnerabilities. I consider successful social work interventions in difficult situations to promote independent lifestyles amongst young people embedded in high levels of abuse, neglect and hostility. I also touch on problems experienced by homeless adults.

Homelessness – a Social Issue, Not a Personal Problem

Legislation defines homelessness primarily as not having a fixed place to sleep during the night. This is an inadequate definition because it does not cover people's wish for a space that they can call home, enjoy their personal lives in and go from and return to at will. Society's treatment of homeless people has generally pathologized them and seen their plight as one of personal failings rather than a social issue that emanates from the social organization of employment opportunities and housing resources. Conceptualizing homelessness as a personal rather than a social issue has allowed the state to ignore cries for assistance except from those deemed worthy of help. Consequently, it provides minimal or residual housing facilities in stigmatized and punitive conditions.

The numbers of homeless people at any one time are difficult to ascertain and often disputed. They vacillate according to social conditions and policies that are enacted. For example, the number of homeless young people aged between 16 and 17 shot up substantially in 1986 when the Tory government removed their housing benefit by changing the Social Security Act. This stance has been retained under New Labour. Nationally, the UK government classifies 10,454 people as 'rough sleepers' who live on the streets and 98,750 in temporary accommodation at the time of writing. These figures exclude nomadic peoples like Gypsies and Travellers and are queried by charities and other organizations that work with homeless people. In the past, homelessness in the UK had been treated as vagrancy and was prohibited by law. People both feared and abused 'vagrants', as people of 'no fixed abode' were called. Many of them were single adult men who moved from place to place looking for work. Local authorities refused to house people if they were from out of their area, and this complicated matters. Lack of income often meant that sleeping rough in fields or other open spaces and going without food were the main options open to 'vagrants'.

The British state did not respond to homelessness in a form other than punishing people until the sixteenth century, when a Poor Law approach was adopted. Within this context, people were given help grudgingly and under strict conditions that required compliance with institutional norms and residency requirements. A chief aim of the policy was to discipline unruly people who were seen as creating difficulties for respectable society. The first of the ensuing housing provisions were called *bridewells*, within which homeless people were expected to learn a trade or profession to keep themselves. These were followed by *workhouses*, where people were expected to work at hard, mind-numbing tasks in return for food and a bed, both of which were of low standard. The workhouse became dreaded and loathed by working-class people. The horrors associated with it still linger in the memories of older generations. Workhouses were followed by the *spike*, or dormitory accommodation provided by local boroughs. These were large impersonal spaces that have more recently been replaced by *hostels*. Hostels often house people with whom practitioners work. Social workers are expected to help homeless people adjust to living in hostel accommodation.

The actions of Shelter and other organizations for homeless people challenged the official view of homelessness as a personal woe or lifestyle choice except for nomadic peoples. During the 1960s, their activism turned homelessness into a social issue by tying it into questions of: affordable housing; social housing provisions at standards that enabled people to retain their human dignity; and earning a decent income to enter the housing market. Shelter was formed as an organization to deal with homelessness amongst the urban population, but quickly realized that there are serious, but often hidden, problems of homelessness in rural areas and so set up SHARC – Shelter's Housing Action in Rural Communities – in 2000 to address the lack of housing for people living in the countryside. Shelter's goal of ending homelessness has not been achieved, but community activists' endeavours on housing resulted in legal challenges during the 1970s and 1980s. These compelled local authorities to provide housing 'fit for human habitation'. Their gains were of limited duration, however, because local authorities started sending people to private sector landlords and bed and breakfast accommodation. Meanwhile, the Thatcher government sold council housing and refused to allow local authorities to invest in replacing the houses sold or refurbish those that were left. The Tories later introduced the Rough Sleepers Initiatives and Homeless Mentally Ill Initiative to manage the problem of 'cardboard cities' in major conurbations, including London. 'Cardboard City' became the term used to describe the habitations of homeless people living on city streets as they sheltered behind cardboard boxes and newspapers, even in severely low temperatures. Their presence shamed a rich nation in the eyes of wealthy visitors, especially those in the capital.

New Labour under Tony Blair continued the tradition of low investments in public housing owned by local authorities. Blair's solution to homelessness was to establish the Rough Sleepers Unit (RSU) with Louise Casey as its head in 1998. It was to reduce substantially the number of rough sleepers, especially in London, by getting them into hostel accommodation, which remains in short supply. Ironically, the RSU increased the number of hostels for homeless people, but reduced bed numbers as better-quality provisions were produced without an increase in overall funds allocated for homeless people. The RSU believed its goal was reached in that its calculations revealed that the number of people sleeping on the streets of the capital fell from 1,850 to 703 between 1998 and 2002. These figures have been disputed by homeless charities, including Shelter. There is a promise of change under Gordon Brown, who is encouraging the construction of 3 million homes, including social housing, by 2020.

This strategy may begin to address some structural issues associated with housing and homelessness that are produced as a consequence of the private market raising house prices to such levels that even professionals like social workers, the police and firefighters struggle to find money to buy homes in London and southeast England, where most jobs are located. London faces additional demands in that tourists and (im)migrants make it their first port of call. The government has not responded to these pressures by providing additional housing resources for short-term use. Instead, it determined that asylum seekers are not entitled to social housing and limited access to this resource by Eastern Europeans who joined the European Union in 2004. This reality makes mockery of Cabinet Minister Margaret Hodge's claim that 'established British families' were being pushed out of social housing by newcomers (Refugee Council, 2006, 2007; Watt, 2007).

The UK is not the only country with structurally caused homelessness. Most English-speaking nations have had similar histories of neglecting homeless people, although welfare benefits for them vary according to country. In the USA, homeless people have less access to welfare assistance than in Britain and many rely on 'panhandling' (begging) and food banks to see them through the day. The composition of homeless groups is of concern in some places. In New York City, half the homeless people are children. This impedes their full development as human beings. In Canada, homelessness and 'panhandling' have been the object of several campaigns aimed at reducing the numbers of those involved and controlling those on drugs or suffering mental ill health who are sleeping on the streets. Homelessness and drug and alcohol misuse are a common combination, making it a 'law and order' issue. This was the case in Vancouver, where 'aggressive panhandling, illegal vending and drug-dealing' were rife, with 3,000 to 4,000 incidents per month recorded in 2004. With the passage of the Safe Street Act that year and the deployment of an additional 33 police officers to patrol the city's streets from September 2006, this figure had dropped to 350 a month in 2007.

Homelessness and Scarcity in Affordable Housing

The reasons people live on the streets are many. Some end up there through reasons beyond their control, arguments with important others and lifestyle choices. The young mother I quote on p. 101 did so because life in the group home was so awful. Other people on the streets through no fault of their own may be there as a result of social neglect. The drama documentary *Cathy Come Home* has become a classic of this genre and depicts social neglect in a powerful way. In the film, town-hall bureaucrats refuse to house homeless families that they define as deliberately becoming homeless to jump the housing queue. Their inaction ultimately leads social workers to take Cathy's children into care. Filmed in 1966, the pertinence of *Cathy Come Home* continues as over 1.5 million people in the UK remain unhoused; many are children and young people.

'Cathy' has become a symbol of social indifference to homeless people, including families with small children. Instead of being housed adequately, as legislation demands, families are lodged in temporary or interim accommodation, usually of the bed-and-breakfast type, where they have to vacate the premises in the morning and wander the streets all day until they are allowed to return in the evening. Housing provided by private landlords can be substandard. Funds come from the public purse, but this provision is expensive as market rents are paid to private landlords. Using general funds for these purposes can strain council budgets. Perth, for example, had a deficit of £350,000 to cover as a result of meeting market rents for social housing. National figures are difficult to access, however, sometimes because appropriate accounts are not kept, as was the case with Shepway District Council, according to the Audit Commission in 2004. Ironically, local authorities drew on private housing more often once substandard council housing was declared 'unfit for human habitation' by court challenges under Section 99 of the 1967 Housing Act. Council house sales under Margaret Thatcher reduced the housing stock under the control of local authorities, increased utilization of private rented and housing association housing to meet their statutory obligations. Being prevented from using money obtained from housing sales for housing purposes further diminishes local authorities' capacity to reduce waiting lists.

British local authorities have dealt with housing shortages by developing waiting lists to accommodate homeless people and prioritizing the needs of those on them. To get on a waiting list, a person or family has to be eligible for housing. This means that they must be 'legally homeless' or not have made themselves intentionally homeless by refusing housing, or leaving accommodation that the council thinks is adequate, regardless of the views of the person living in it, and be 'habitually resident' in the UK, i.e., this is where they normally live. They have to prove residency unless they hold refugee status. To get on a waiting list, people have to be in priority need: pregnant women; having dependent children; having special needs; or becoming homeless through a natural disaster like flooding. People on these lists endure lengthy waits that can stretch to years for the limited accommodation at a council's disposal.

A local authority can discharge its obligations through temporary housing, which may lengthen the period before a person or family is adequately and permanently housed. This unsatisfactory solution to the problem has recently been aggravated by media campaigns that pit the housing needs of refugees and non-nationals residing in the UK with legitimate claims to housing against those of people who have spent years on the housing list. Attention-grabbing headlines in the press about immigrants getting council housing over local residents intensify friction around both groups' justifiable claims to scarce social resources (Dodd and Wintour, 2005, 2006). The problem of scarce low-cost housing must be resolved by building more affordable, high-quality dwellings.

Rarely do public discussions about homelessness ask whether we should have housing waiting lists in a wealthy country like the UK. Waiting lists for homeless people ration what housing is available. The market privileges those who can afford to pay, including those with sufficient means to purchase second homes for leisure purposes alongside a primary one for daily living. Social housing remains in scarce supply and unable to respond to human need in this sphere. Whether Gordon Brown's refreshing intention of building affordable housing will change the situation remains to be seen. Homelessness indicates how social policies create social problems that social workers are then asked to solve, often with limited resources for doing so. Thus, they are restricted to offering: temporary shelter; advice in getting on waiting lists; assistance in applying for social housing and welfare benefits; counselling; and their skills as lobbyists for policy changes.

Multiple Problems and Life on the Streets

Homeless people are likely to experience a number of social problems. These include: financial insecurity; social isolation; separation from families; poor physical and mental health; and lack of suitable accommodation. Their lives can be cut short as they fall victims to street violence, drug abuse, crime and prostitution. Their neglect by society is a form of institutional abuse because their need for accommodation and health resources could be met if society chose to make these available. As the

RSU approach indicates, social responses to homeless people favour taking them off the streets. They become invisible statistics as they sleep on the floors or sofas of kind individuals, including family and friends who offer them limited space; or sneak into derelict or abandoned buildings to shelter from the elements (crucial in winter). Homelessness is not simply a problem of urban living. It occurs in rural streets, where it is more invisible and less likely to hit the headlines than it is in urban areas.

The popular depiction of the local tramp drinking meths and sleeping rough on a park bench is the iconic portrait of a homeless person. This portrayal ignores the structural impact of shortages in affordable housing on their situations and makes it easier to blame individuals for their plight. Research has established that significant numbers of homeless people have drug and alcohol problems – 80 per cent of homeless people are regular users of these substances, but only 3 per cent seek detox facilities. Half of homeless people experience mental ill health and are over-represented in these statistics. There is enormous variety in their needs, and instability in their housing position identifies the lack of appropriate facilities to cater for a mobile population. Drug Action Teams (DATs) are responsible for communicating with all drug service providers in an area and ensuring that they meet the needs of homeless people. But services are not ring-fenced and needs are poorly served. Social workers are members of DATs and help to deliver treatment services. They also support homeless people in applying for social housing, assist families with children to move from inappropriate accommodation, and lobby for decent alternatives to current housing options.

Many of those on the streets have been released from care, 'looked after' children or young people whose life chances are much reduced. They are more likely to be in trouble with the law than are other children and perform less well at school. Poor school performance leads to disadvantage in the job market and unemployment, seriously jeopardizing their quality of life in future. These young people may have poor relationships with their parents or other family members, and so social networks based on kin relations and wider social groupings are often absent from their lives. This disadvantages the social support networks that those in different circumstances can take for granted. A variety of social workers – youth workers, community workers, social care workers or volunteers – work with them through outreach programmes to provide accommodation, usually of a temporary nature, and food. They also link them up to other services. For young people this can include relatives, school and health services. Social workers can also help them find employment.

Although isolated from wider society, these young people can form good relationships with others on the street and create surrogate families and networks of support where they 'look after each other'. One such young person claimed:

> It was a real family environment with all the other street kids. We took care of each other and supported each other and did criminal acts together. . . . I . . . felt more of a connection and safer and happier with them [on the streets] than I did in the group home. (Dominelli et al., 2005).

This young person's experiences indicate that homeless people form significant relationships with each other and form a street family where care, nurturing and support are offered, with no strings attached. These friendships become essential in dealing with otherwise difficult situations on the street and enable young people to survive in circumstances where they might otherwise fail. Social workers can pick up on these strengths to redirect their energies and prepare for their futures.

How Homeless People Resist Stereotypes of Their Capacities

Many homeless young people survive on the margins of society, living a hand-to-mouth existence on the streets. People encountering them feel embarrassed and will avoid eye contact if they are begging. Homeless people demonstrate strengths and resilience that enable them to get through the day. Social workers can build on these skills. John Bird set up the *Big Issue* to enable those living on the streets to sell a newspaper as merchandise to earn money while retaining their dignity and pride. The *Big Issue* hit the British streets in 1991 as a monthly magazine/newspaper. Increased circulation allowed it to be published forthnightly in 1992 and weekly in 1993. The *Big Issue* Foundation was formed in 1995 to advance the interests of homeless people. Promoting self-sufficiency rather than relying on state handouts has been integrated into welfare state ideology and popularized by Tony Blair's slogan 'hand-up not a handout'.

Homelessness is experienced differently by diverse groups of people: one in six of those sleeping rough is under age 25; one in four is over 60. A gender analysis reveals that one in ten homeless people is a woman. Those with few social resources, including social networks and kin relations, may find that they have little choice in how to resolve their homelessness. Those with significant networks may be offered accommodation of some sort, albeit on a temporary basis that may include sleeping on a sofa at a friend's house so that they can stay off the streets. A drawback to this solution is that British local authorities may refuse a housing application unless the person can show that they have been evicted from such accommodation through no fault of their own.

In the case study below, I present some of the complicated issues that young homeless women, particularly those with black minority ethnic origins, encounter and have to deal with, often with social work support that fails to meet their specific needs, and consider how poor practice with homeless young people could be improved.

Case study: The struggles of a homeless young woman of Nigerian descent

Malika was a 14-year-old girl of Hausa (Nigerian) descent born in Leicester. She had been taken into residential care at her request when she was 12 because her Muslim parents refused to let her go out with her school friends after she had reached puberty and she was constantly arguing with them and being disciplined for insolence. After being received into care, she refused to have anything to do with her parents, extended family or other members of the Muslim community. The social workers she approached were white and did not know her culture or understand its significance to her. They felt that she simply wanted to live like any other white teenager. When her parents tried to contact her, they said she did not wish to speak to them. This was true, but the social workers made no attempt at reconciliation or encouraging Malika to talk to her parents on the phone.

Malika absconded from the home when she was 14 because she felt badly bullied by the white English residents. She escaped by catching a train to London. She had no friends and no money in the city. She was hanging about King's Cross station when an older Asian man saw her. He started talking to her and when it became clear that she was on her own (she told him she had been recently orphaned in a car crash), he offered her food and a bed for the night.

Malika accepted and went to his house in Brixton, where he introduced her to several friends as his 18-year-old 'niece' who was visiting him from Uganda. He asked her to call him 'Babu'. Malika initially went along with the story and was grateful for being housed and fed. She felt no need to go out and stayed indoors all day watching television. After a week of being at his house, 'Babu' brought some friends home. They started to play cards and drink late into the night. The same thing happened the next day and they asked Malika to join them, which she did. Later when they all went to bed for the night, she was followed into her bedroom and raped by one of them. She was unsure which one it was, but when she challenged them the next morning, all denied touching her and told her she had made the story up because she had drunk excessively. She tried to escape, but all the doors and windows were locked.

She started crying and demanded to be let free. 'Babu' refused, saying that she would get into serious trouble on the streets in London, where she knew no one. He added that if she misbehaved he would call the social workers, who would take her back to the home she had left, or, even worse, her parents (she had by this stage admitted they lived in northern England). She could stay, but he was a poor man and he could not afford to keep her in his house without being paid. But he would not let her go out to work. He suggested that she satisfy his friends, who would pay for her sexual favours, and that would be a way of her earning her keep. This she refused to do. One evening, a few days after this conversation, 'Babu' began to smoke cannabis and offered her some. She tried it and found that she liked it. Before long, he had her trying harder drugs, including heroin, along with booze, and wanting more. But he would not give her any unless she did what he asked.

At this point he also started to abuse her sexually under the guise of being madly in love with her. Eventually, he expected her to have sex with other men who paid him when she was 'high' (relaxed and contented) on heroin. If she did not comply, he would beat her. Malika knew about the addictive nature of heroin and tried to control her desire for it. It was easier to do this if 'Babu' did not demand sex from her. This abuse continued for six months before 'Babu' got careless and forgot to lock the window in his room before going out for the day, as was his habit. Malika was never told where he went. On this occasion, Malika saw that the window was unlocked, and although she had no coat and only a pair of slippers for shoes, she jumped out into the pouring rain. She fell about five feet into the garden, but except for a few bumps and bruises she was not hurt. She ran from the place as fast as she could and got on a bus.

She had only five pounds and a small amount of cannabis resin on her that she had managed to hide from 'Babu', and she went from bus to bus to get as far away from his place as possible. She ended up outside Paddington station and began to wander around to see what she could find to eat. She saw a half-eaten sandwich that someone had left and slipped it in her pocket. She found a cup of cold coffee that she took as well. She felt frozen, but her clothes had dried out on the buses and it had now stopped raining. That night, she huddled in a doorway in a hut behind a restaurant, shivering with cold, hugging herself to keep warm and sharing with stray cats the scraps left by diners. As dawn broke the next morning, she knew she had to move on. But she did not know where to go or what to do. She wandered around aimlessly and hungry for hours. Just as she reached the point of exhaustion towards evening, she spotted a hostel for homeless young people and went in to ask for a place for the night. She told them she had just arrived in London and had nowhere to stay.

The struggle to find shelter in a safe and nurturing environment is one commonly faced by young people who for whatever reason end up on the streets. Addressing the range of needs that Malika displays requires a multi-disciplinary team that can handle cultural issues and substance misuse. Malika's story is a tragic one of betrayal by those responsible for her care and well-being. There are a number of narratives in her life. These are of the: care system failing a young woman; abuse of a vulnerable young woman by predator adults; family breakdown; Malika's resilience, her desire to survive and look after herself in extremely difficult circumstances; and the social isolation and limited opportunities for autonomous growth that the adult world provides for young people like her.

From the very start, Malika had been placed in a vulnerable position by social workers because they did not comply with the requirements of the 1989 Children Act (Sec. 22(5)) to provide for her cultural and religious needs. She should not have been placed in a home where her unique identity and needs were ignored. The social workers and residential workers responsible for her care should have picked up on the bullying that she was experiencing, again because she was different, dealt with the perpetrators, and helped Malika address its impact on her. They should have assisted her in working through her relationship with her parents and community instead of assuming a complete rupture was what she wanted.

Malika's vulnerability as a young woman made her a target for predator adults, who are constantly on the look-out for young people, especially homeless young women without money, to abuse sexually and exploit. 'Babu' was committing criminal offences by having sex with an under-age young woman, encouraging others to do so, misusing Class 'A' drugs and living off immoral earnings. As he was still at large, he remained a danger to other young people and should have been picked up by the police and charged with these offences. Whether any of these matters would be addressed would depend on whether social workers at the hostel would be sensitive enough to probe Malika's superficial presentation of her situation and work with her in a culturally appropriate and person-centred manner. It would have been their responsibility to ensure that this occurred. Doing so would have been essential if she were not to be further abused by the system. To engage with Malika as a whole person, social workers would have to cease acting as techno-bureaucrats. Techno-bureaucrats are professionals who respond to a situation within the parameters of a technical rationality driven by checklists that tackle only the superficialities that a person asking for services chooses to present. They are often overworked and have little time to probe beneath surface realities.

A major theme in Malika's story is that of uncertainty in most aspects of her life – in family relations, friendships, education, housing and employment prospects. Lack of certainty or predictability in her social circumstances placed her at risk and made her easy prey for adults determined to take advantage of her vulnerabilities. Her uncertain position provided the fluid structure in which those who lack a moral compass, like 'Babu', could exploit her wish for a secure, certain and safe environment. Ulrich Beck (1992, 1999), who coined the term the 'risk society', warns that it is impossible to find certainty in contemporary life. This makes Malika's search for it illusory. Beck suggests that dealing with uncertainty requires 'reflexive modernity' and characterizes survival strategies in modern lives. No one helped Malika to explore and critique her representations of herself, and so the opportunity to be critically reflexive and learn about herself and her deepest needs was lost. Malika's attempt to escape her circumstances – leaving her family, residential care and 'Babu''s house – could be construed as an exercise in resilience and reflexivity, albeit one that took her from one risky situation to another.

This is because she always sought a practical response to her plight and never probed beyond its immediacy. A sensitive social worker or counsellor able to empathize with her, highlight her skills and resilience and start from where she was at could have helped her acquire this knowledge.

Uncertainty also features in professional practice. According to Nigel Parton (1998), uncertainty and ambiguity incapacitate social workers who look for certainty where none is possible. I have argued that uncertainty has been a consistent element in professional practice, not least because social workers can never expect to have full knowledge of a situation or system at their disposal. They cannot control service users to the extent necessary to prevent them from acting according to what they want to do or think is appropriate but may be illegal. Social workers have to take action in situations that might include rejecting service users' wishes. Acting to take decisions presupposes a degree of certainty, however temporary. Instead of conceptualizing the issue as a binary one of certainty versus uncertainty, it might help to consider what social workers do as uncertain certainty. Dealing with *un*certainty in change processes encourages social workers continuously to evaluate their practice and take corrective measures that seem appropriate. Jan Fooks (2002) terms this constant evaluation and re-evaluation of social work interventions 'critical reflexivity'. Critical reflexivity enables professionals to critique their own practice and be held accountable by others for what they do or do not do. Demands for greater accountability have been central in service users' demands for non-oppressive practice since they began to challenge the infallibility of professional expertise rooted in decontextualized practice during the 1960s. Critical reflexivity helps social workers intervene in more empowering ways.

Conclusions

Homeless people provide social workers with complex situations that require inter-professional partnerships to bring together the extensive range of knowledge required for effective interventions. Critical reflexivity in social workers' approach will facilitate their engaging with homeless people (or other service users) as human beings with the capacity to decide how they want to lead their lives and respond with assistance that homeless people require – housing, health services, education, jobs and welfare benefits. If they choose homelessness as a lifestyle choice, it is inappropriate for social workers to compel them to settle, as happened to Roma peoples, Gypsies and Travellers. Social workers can support homeless people's desire for independent living and challenge society's neglect of their plight. Arguing that society must quickly address structural problems associated with scarcity in affordable housing provides fertile ground for social workers to act as advocates. They can also uphold homeless people's rights as users of mental health, employment or education services.

7

People Who Misuse Substances

Addictions or Responses to Difficult Life Circumstances and Relationships?

A wide spectrum of people engage in substance misuse, including alcohol and other drugs of various kinds. They engage in a broad range of activities which are linked to self-harm and offences against others. Important in the latter regard are burglary and violence against people to fund drug habits. Drug users are responsible for around half the crime that takes place in the UK. Crime linked to Class 'A' drugs has been estimated to cost Britain around £18 billion per year (Gordon, 2006).

Poverty, lack of social roles, poor relationships with important others and difficult life circumstances often cause people to misuse substances. Social work interventions in the lives of those who abuse substances concentrate largely on symptoms and not causes. This occurs because it is simpler to focus on addressing measurable or easily quantified outcomes – e.g., the number of days that an individual receiving support remains drug-free – than on repairing social relationships, dealing with structural inequalities or enhancing self-esteem. Many of those misusing substances have endured fragmented, difficult and abusive relationships that have damaged their sense of self-worth and sent them spiralling downwards into conditions that can be worse than those they left. They experience a sense of camaraderie and belonging in relating to others who abuse substances that they have not realized elsewhere. This can draw them back into disastrous relationships, even when they know that these can damage their well-being, because they feel safer in these than out of them. For people who misuse substances, functioning adequately may be a temporary state. In abusing substances, they risk irreparable damage to their health and even death.

In this chapter, I examine substance misuse including solvents, alcohol and hard drugs, using case study materials to show that different kinds of professionals, and not just social workers, intervene in the lives of people who misuse substances. These include professionals in health care, probation, the police, judiciary and volunteers, working together to deliver appropriate services. I consider inter-agency working, a major challenge in these professional relationships, in terms of what service users deem is most helpful. Agency exigencies can dominate the interventions offered and disadvantage service users by not giving them precisely the treatment they need at a given point in time. There is considerable controversy about how best to help drug addicts. Politicians reflect these ambiguities, with some feeling that drug users should be imprisoned for breaking the law. Others argue that therapeutic interventions that address their needs would more effectively reduce drug use in the longer term.

Drug Classification and Use

Drugs can be used for recreational purposes, therapy or illegal activities. Drugs have a long history of recreational use, for enjoyment, relief from debilitating pain, and in religious rituals, e.g., ganja in the Rastafarian religion. To support those misusing substances, social workers should understand the substances and treatments available. Drug classification reflects the ambiguities evident in usage because some drugs are helpful allies in medical treatments as well as being highly addictive substances that alter moods and/or state of mind. Drugs are roughly classified as legal or illegal – 'illicit' in the jargon. Some, like cannabis, that are illegal for private use can be legally prescribed for various ailments. Given under medical control, cannabis can alleviate suffering caused by debilitating and chronic pain. This ambiguity has resulted in various drugs increasingly becoming part of the social landscape. Usage has varied over the years, with recreational drug use catching on across a wide segment of the British population during the 1980s. Drug use is becoming more socially acceptable, despite knowledge of serious side-effects, dangers to the users' health and heartaches caused to friends and relatives when usage leads to criminal activity and/or death.

Howard Parker et al. (1998) have termed the growing acceptability of higher levels of drug use, especially among young people, the 'normalization thesis'. The perception of these substances as recreational drugs or those used on a casual basis contributes to their normalization, despite their illicitness in law. Their 'normalized' status has resulted in a wider cross-section of the British public being involved in illicit drug use and intensified pressure for their legalization. Its supporters' arguments revolve around recreational usage not being the same as addiction. They claim drug addiction impairs social and physical functioning. Recreational use does not produce these side-effects. People who support recreational usage perceive casual recreational use as falling within acceptable norms, but consider dependent daily drug use inappropriate.

Drug classification in the UK is governed by the 1971 Misuse of Drugs Act. This identified psychoactive substances that were classified Class 'A' to 'C' according to the potential of the substance to harm individuals or society. Those available for medicinal use were classified as Schedule 1 to 5. Those known as Class 'A' drugs, like heroin, cocaine, ecstasy and now crystal meth, are highly addictive and dangerous to health. Class 'B' drugs covered barbiturates, amphetamines, codeine and cannabis resin. Class 'C' drugs included mild amphetamines, anabolic steroids and minor tranquillizers. Schedule 1 drugs covered heroin, ecstasy and cocaine, while Schedule 5 focused on over-the-counter remedies like cough medicines and painkillers. The 1971 Act has been amended in the intervening period, with drugs being added to it as government has thought appropriate, e.g., gammahydroxybutytate (GHB), otherwise known as the 'date drug', and, in 2002, the addition of anabolic steroids as Class 'C' drugs. Classification is important in determining the severity of court sentences for those convicted of (mis)use and in planning treatment regimes.

Heroin is an opiate or analgesic drug taken for relaxation and contentment, but it can cause depression as well as being seriously addictive. Opiates are Class 'A' drugs and have a calming effect on individuals. Moreover, a person's body becomes tolerant of them and requires more of the substance to achieve the same effect as earlier in a drug career. Ecstasy is a stimulant that can make people who are already depressed even more so. The hallucinogen lysergic acid diethylamide (LSD), advocated by 'hippie guru' Timothy Leary in the 1960s, was associated with the subcultural mantra of 'Turn on; Tune in; Drop Out'. Leary's advocacy of the drug was linked to critiques of capitalist consumer society,

which was seen to have failed to meet the needs of the majority population, but this downplayed the fact that it can give rise to serious side-
effects, such as unpredictable mood swings, delusions and hallucinations,
on top of physical symptoms that include muscle weakness and sleepless-
ness. Each of these drugs can cause severe withdrawal symptoms and
requires medical assistance in ending its (mis)use. Each has a withdrawal
regime and voluntary organizations to support those wanting to stop.
For example, methadone, a synthetic opioid developed in Germany in
1937, has been used medically as an analgesic or painkiller employed to
manage chronic pain but also as a way of weaning people off narcotic
addiction. This latter application is popular for heroin withdrawal and
is part of a 'substitution therapy'. Its use is controversial, however, as
methadone, also a Class 'A' drug, can itself be addictive, making it
problematic both for managing chronic pain and as a heroin substitute.
I consider the effects of popularly abused drugs below.

The emergence of HIV/AIDS further complicates issues of drug use,
especially when users share needles to inject. The attempt to convince
intravenous drug users not to share needles to avoid catching HIV/AIDS
or hepatitis B and C has led to 'needle exchange schemes' where old
needles are exchanged for new ones. Another scheme is the use of Arrest
Referral Schemes (ARSs), whereby the opportunity to begin working to
end drug use is provided at the point of arrest. ARSs do not stay the
process of law, but help those wishing to end their addiction begin the
difficult process of doing so under supported conditions. ARSs contribute
to the debate of shifting drug policy towards treating rather than simply
punishing offenders. Money devoted to these is limited. Only 13 per cent
of the funds the British government spends on drugs goes on treatment
and rehabilitation, with a further 12 per cent on education and prevention. The 1998 Crime and Disorder Act brought Drug Treatment and
Testing Orders (DTTOs) into being to facilitate an offender's access to
treatment. DTTOs provide a drug user with intensive treatment involving many professionals, including those in social work, health, the criminal justice system and education working together. DTTO usage has
risen to the extent that more money is spent on drug treatments in prison
than in the community (Turning Point, 2004). Yet, despite this, 47,000
prisoners in British jails still need detox services.

Crystal Meth

Crystal meth, the popular name for methamphetamine, is a recent addition to the addictive drugs repertoire. It is highly addictive and can be

smoked, snorted or injected. Crystal meth causes long-term damage to the brain by attacking the small blood vessels and can lead to stroke. Meth alters the brain's production of dopamine and can cause a person to become depressed when the drug's effect wears off. This depression can last a long time and the blocked release of dopamine can cause anhedonia, or a state of mind where people fail to find anything that makes them feel pleasure. It can be of long duration in adolescents, who are more difficult to treat than adults. It can initiate psychosis (paranoia or delusions) that persist even if a person stops using the drug. Regular physical activity creates endorphins which alleviate the symptoms of anhedonia, and those coming off the drug are encouraged to participate in physical activities, including games that require group involvement, to reduce its effects. Regular use of crystal meth damages concentration by impairing attention span, causes loss of memory, reduces impulse control and limits learning functions.

Crystal meth inflames the lining of the heart, thus storing up trouble in this organ. Overdoses can cause death through extreme elevated body temperatures, convulsions and cardiovascular collapse or heart failure. Crystal meth causes tooth decay, and the corrosive chemicals it contains cause irreparable damage to the lining of the nose. Risks of contracting HIV, hepatitis B and C and other blood-borne viruses increase if the drug is injected. Sexual dysfunction is another side-effect. During 'highs', young people can become extremely violent, especially if working in gangs, and become involved in disturbances of group-based violent behaviour called 'swarming'.

Once usage of meth begins, there is a 'high' and 'crash' pattern that has the user requiring more and more of the substance to return to 'normal'. This leads to loss of control over drug usage and the addiction. Withdrawal can be difficult, and symptoms can include excess sleepiness, increased appetite and depression lasting from seven to ten days. Difficulties in sleeping, short-term memory loss and reduced concentration span last much longer. Treatment includes a period of stabilization through detoxication and acute withdrawal, and a considerable period of counselling or psychotherapy in either outpatient or residential clinics. Mutual support groups and cognitive-behavioural therapies (CBTs) can help. CBTs assist users to change their behaviour by identifying negative thought patterns and moving their thinking in positive directions. Prevention strategies can be taught through schools or outreach settings and involve workers from education welfare or community workers – the social workers practising in these locations.

People can self-refer for treatment or be proposed by professionals or concerned individuals. Several models are used in dealing with meth users. The matrix model is popular in Vancouver, Canada. It combines a number of different methods to stimulate users into coming off the substance. Another method is contingency management. This is based on a reward system – a bit like behaviour modification – that provides an incentive for a person who is addicted to continue treatment. The reward is usually tailored to the specific individual and requires the therapist or health professional to figure out what might work for a particular person.

Ecstasy

The stimulant drug ecstasy or methylenedioxymetamine (MDMA), is a synthetic amphetamine-based drug, used in raves and clubs because it produces a 'high' that lifts a person's moods. It is one of the four most commonly used drugs in the USA, along with cocaine, heroin and cannabis. Ecstasy was a 'love drug' of the 1960s. Its recreational use began in the 1980s after psychotherapist Leo Zeff showed that it enhanced communication, increased introspection and reduced psychological inhibitions. It is not as addictive as other Class 'A' drugs, but has serious short-term side-effects like increased heart palpitations, reduced appetite and memory loss. It also causes long-term damage to nerve cells in the brain and increases blood pressure, which can give rise to cardiovascular problems.

Using amphetamines ('speed'), methadrine or drinking alcohol along with ecstasy worsens its effects. The drug can also lead to severe dehydration, the countering of which led to the death through water intoxication of Leah Betts, a British teenager, in 1995 while clubbing after she had taken one ecstasy tablet. She had obtained the 'E', as it is also called, from a friend – someone she trusted, and not an unknown dealer who was only interested in her money. Her parents have used her death to warn other young people of the dangers of overheating and dehydrating when taking ecstasy. Leah's case suggests there is no such thing as a safe drug, a safe amount to take or safe conditions in which to take it, although 'E' users claim that these conditions can be met. The problem highlighted by the inquest into Leah's death was that teenagers can drink too much water in trying to address dehydration, which most of them know is a side-effect of ecstasy. The number of tablets taken, the amount of water drunk, the person's weight and general physical health are amongst the range of factors that can affect the outcome, and that's why the simple message of drinking water is inadequate in mitigating its potentially lethal effect.

Solvent Abuse

Solvent Abuse or Volatile Substance Abuse (VSA) is linked to the abuse of everyday articles ranging from petrol and paint thinners to adhesives to get a 'high'. Intoxication on solvents can lead to drowsiness, confusion and aggressive or accident-prone actions. Abusing solvents has detrimental effects on health. The habit causes one person a week to die from engaging in this behaviour, usually from cardiac arrest. Butane gas is the solvent most frequently involved in these cases. One-third of these are first-time users. Many are young children. The largest group of solvent abusers are aged 14 to 18. The Society for the Prevention of Solvent and Volatile Substance Abuse (Re-Solv) is a major supporter of those seeking to break this form of addiction.

Socially Acceptable Drugs and Addiction: Alcohol Addiction

Alcohol is a drug and addictive. Despite concerns about teenage 'binge drinking', specifically damaging the liver and disruptive behaviour on Britain's streets, it is socially acceptable to drink alcohol. Rarely is it presented as an addictive drug that people should stay away from, although teetotallers do. Some people believe that alcohol addiction is not as serious as addiction to other drugs. This is not necessarily so. Alcohol misuse can have devastating consequences for individuals and families. These range from disruptive behaviour involving violence against the person to death through accidents, alcohol poisoning or cancer of the liver. Many people addicted to alcohol deny these outcomes, thus creating additional problems in getting treatment.

Alcoholics Anonymous (AA) was created as a self-help initiative whereby those who have been or are addicted can assist those currently addicted. It advocates a policy of abstinence. The AA is a key voluntary organization that helps people wanting to end their alcohol abuse. It is run for and by members who have previously misused alcohol and follows a scheme known as the '12 Steps Programme' in terminating alcohol addiction. The Programme was begun in the United States in 1935 by Bill Wilson, a stockbroker, and Robert Smith, a surgeon. Their consumption of alcohol had risen out of control, but they found that talking to each other about their problems helped reduce it. They realized that they could use these discussions to end their own addiction and help others. They created the 12 Steps Programme to enable people to recognize the interconnected nature of their problems and focus on living healthier lives.

Some people become addicted to both alcohol and drugs. This is known as the 'dual drag'. Between 30 and 50 per cent of those on 'dual drag' have mental health problems, including those of becoming confused and finding it difficult to get housing. Phoenix House, started by Professor Griffith Edwards in 1970 as a residential rehabilitation centre in south London for those suffering dual addictions, was based on the American Phoenix House, a self-help therapeutic community that inspired him to use a structured environment to initiate changes in lifestyles amongst those who misused substances and help them to take control of their lives. The charity has since expanded throughout the UK and is now involved in community, prison-based and residential rehabilitation services. It changed its name to Phoenix Futures in November 2006 to reflect its extended provisions and also its aim of transforming the lives of those who abuse substances and enabling them to secure for themselves a better future. Release UK, a specialist service on drugs and the law, began in 1967 to support and advise drug users and their families and professionals working with them. It produced 'bust cards', telling people about their rights during police raids. (People caught by the police were 'busted', hence the term 'bust' cards.) It also offers a legal helpline (the first in the world) and a heroin helpline. Its services are confidential and non-judgemental.

The 'War on Drugs'

The drug trade is a multi-billion dollar industry that crosses borders, despite its illegality, and covers the production, distribution and supply of these substances. Organized crime syndicates are often involved in these activities. Their tentacles have a wide reach that sweeps many people into a global net with a hierarchy that leaves those at the top earning fortunes. Respectable people and businesses are drawn into these webs as these criminals seek 'clean' outlets to 'launder' their 'dirty' money and hide the source of their ill-gotten wealth. A number of Western countries have sought to intervene in these situations by confiscating the assets of those convicted of drug offences, particularly those linked to producing and/or supplying drugs. The attempts to cut drug production, distribution and supply have led to a set of interventions that have been termed the 'war on drugs' and involve international law enforcement agencies cooperating with each other to apprehend these 'traders'.

The debate about what approach society and law enforcement agencies in the criminal justice system should take towards drug users has been long-standing. However, a solution that reduces the acceptability of drug use or the incidence of crime associated with sustaining the habit has not been found. On the more punitive side, responses to drugs have been highly influenced by the American 'war on drugs' initiated by President Ronald Reagan in the 1980s and continued by subsequent presidents. Its adherents advocate 'zero tolerance' on drugs and the prosecution of all infringements of the law, no matter how minor. This position ignores its implications for the population as a whole, given the large numbers of people at the lower levels of drug use, including recreational usage that might be criminalized as a result of this approach. British attitudes to drugs have hardened during the intervening period, and the demise of the treatment of heroin addicts by supplying their wants through the NHS has resulted in a growth in numbers.

British doctors prescribed heroin from the 1920s to 1960s and managed to control its use and purchase through the shadow or illicit economy. This typically British approach in controlling the misuse of drugs by treating it as a medical problem goes back to the Rolleston Committee of 1924–6, which argued for the use of the medical model in reducing consumption by those addicted to drugs. This had a preventative element in that it created an alternative supply of drugs through the GP's surgery, albeit for those seeking to 'kick the habit'. It also reduced the profit margins of those supplying through the illicit market. The withdrawal of support for drug users through NHS auspices has been paralleled by an increase in illicit use, and drug offences have risen in consequence. The number of drug offenders rose from 500 in 1926 to 26,000 in 1987 and 104,000 in 2000. Actual drug use is difficult to determine, and these figures are disputed. The British Crime Survey, for example, reports much lower levels of illicit drug use than self-report studies conducted in schools.

In Britain, using drugs for pain relief has lent force to arguments that drugs like cannabis should be re-classified as Class 'C' rather than 'B' because they are not highly damaging to health. This, the latest move in a long debate on the topic, began in 2002, and cannabis became reclassified as a Class 'C' drug in 2004. Its use to alleviate pain in medical conditions such as arthritis has intensified arguments for its decriminalization for personal consumption. People's willingness to act on this basis is reflected in crime statistics that show that 67 per cent of those cautioned or convicted of unlawful possession of cannabis had it for their personal use, with only small amounts of the substance being seized during arrest.

The Blair government responded to the decriminalization drive on cannabis by asking the police not to prosecute people for possession of small quantities of cannabis if it were only for personal use. This was a far cry from decriminalization, but even this approach was strongly resisted by Keith Hellawell, popularly referred to as Tony Blair's 'Drug Tsar', who resigned in 2002 because he opposed the government's lax attitude towards cannabis. Counter-demands for the restoration of Class 'B' status for cannabis are currently being mooted, indicating that the debate on the best way to respond to cannabis usage is far from over. Politicians continue to reject the demand for changing the classification of ecstasy from Class 'A' to Class 'B'. The 'politics' of drug use and misuse are complicated and the 'war on drugs' can be applied in ways not conducive to ridding the streets of the presence or (mis)use of dangerous drugs.

A lenient approach to cannabis has been argued in some Western countries for several decades. A Canadian government commission exploring the dangers of cannabis recommended in the 1960s that it be decriminalized. The government has not accepted this finding. Pressure from religious groups and successive American administrations that deem Canadian laws on drug use already lax have played a major role in ensuring this outcome. Lack of clarity and ambiguity amongst researchers as to the precise impact of different drugs on human behaviour confounds decision-makers. Evidence about the harmful effects of drugs has been disputed as drug experts line up on both sides of the argument, making it difficult for individuals to judge what constitute appropriate responses. Their distinction between mind-altering drugs and mood-enhancing drugs is rather blurred for most purposes. In the UK, the Runciman Recommendations of 2001 suggested decriminalizing cannabis, ecstasy and LSD and creating a new offence of supplying small amounts to friends without making money.

The Netherlands is the country seen as having the most tolerant policy on drugs. It draws a distinction between hard and soft drugs and had between 25,000 and 28,000 registered addicts in 2006. This compared to 150,000 for the UK – around one and a half times as many as a proportion of the population. In the Netherlands, hard drugs are strongly controlled and policed, while soft drugs are tolerated. Those known to be addicted to drugs receive free treatment through the Dutch national health system. The Netherlands has been the prime example of a country that has taken a tolerant approach to cannabis with 'cafés' where people over 18 can sit in comfortable surroundings and enjoy a 'smoke'. The café owners are limited in the amount of drugs they can have on the premises and this is rigorously policed. If they were caught with more than the regulation amount, they would lose their licence.

Café owners claim that the amount they are allowed to hold cannot meet demand. They feel that the distinction between possession and producing the drug is becoming nonsensical and want people to be permitted to grow their own cannabis plants. This view is supported by Dutch people. Research from the Netherlands indicates that this more leisured approach to drugs is a safer way of controlling the side-effects of drug use than leaving it to take place on the streets. The Netherlands' tolerance of cannabis has been challenged by European countries that take a tougher stance on drugs. They argue that 'drug tourism' attracts large numbers of their nationals and they want the cafés closed. Overseas visitors have strained the Dutch system as there are insufficient drugs in cafés to cater for them. Their presence is highly problematic in towns like Rotterdam and Maastricht that have become enmeshed in a global market for drugs.

Despite the 'war on drugs', problems remain. The link between drug use and crime is strong. Feeding an addictive habit can lead to crime, especially household burglaries, being committed as the drive to secure more drugs for the next 'high' becomes all-consuming and an individual's disposable funds for drugs dwindle. Drug dealing has become a profitable if unlawful occupation; drug users can be drawn into its orbit to secure their next 'hit'. Others enjoy consumer advantages attached to a seemingly lucrative lifestyle. But many drug dealers live in squalid conditions; their aspirations to wealth, grandeur and security remain mirages in an unreachable distance.

Drug Misuse, Recreational Drug Consumption and Social Work Practice

Statutory social workers intervene in substance misuse situations involving children; voluntary workers with those wishing to stop misusing; and probation officers with convicted drug users serving sentences for drug offences. Social workers who work with those misusing substances are more likely to be employed in voluntary sector agencies that support the rehabilitation efforts of those addicted. The courts can order drug rehabilitation as a part of a sentence involving Drug Treatment and Testing Orders (DTTOs) that probation officers monitor. Their effectiveness since their establishment in 1998 is unproven. Michael Hough et al.'s (2003) finding of 80 per cent reconviction rates for drug-using offenders on DTTOs is similar to the reconviction rates for other offenders.

As drug consumption spreads, professionals are also represented amongst users. Social workers are now increasingly found amongst those who have used or are using drugs on an occasional basis or for medical purposes. This can affect their views on drug use, their responses to those who take them and their capacity to work with those misusing them. They may experience role conflict and ethical dilemmas. For example, can drug-using social workers respond effectively to drug-using parents with small children in their care? Will their answers to questions about the extent to which drug use can be tolerated in parents with young children be appropriate? Should they even be working with such cases? Should they be social workers? Will they be better or worse practitioners as a result of personal knowledge about drug use? Regardless of a social worker's usage, these are serious questions because research has shown that the consequences for children raised by drug-misusing parents can be dire. These concerns are being addressed in a context where controversy about drug use and its capacity to impair judgements is hotly disputed. The General Social Care Council suggests that drug-taking behaviour is deleterious for social worker registration.

Not over-reacting to recreational drug use or under-reacting to problematic drug use is a balance that social workers intervening in such situations have to find. Guidelines for drug-using parents have been published by the Standing Conference on Drug Abuse (SCODA), now called Drug Scope since 1987. It advises social workers to go for 'good enough parenting' as the 'norm' in examining parental fitness to care for children. Harm reduction strategies and working within Department of Health (DH, 2007) guidance help address the diverse needs that accompany substance misuse.

Other ethical dilemmas social workers encounter in practice stem from requirements in the 1989 Children Act. This obliges social workers to keep children with parents wherever possible, using the criteria of what is in the 'best interests of the child' in reaching a decision. Social workers who form working partnerships with drug-using parents have to address complexity when assessing the risk they pose to children and make fine judgements about whether children will be safe if left with them. Social workers can focus on drug consumption rather than production and involvement in selling drugs to determine whether parents will provide the care that children need. They proceed along these lines on the grounds that the parents' ability to control their consumption is the most crucial consideration in assessing their capacity to look after children. Misjudgements in this area can have disastrous consequences for children, as it did for Toni-Ann Byfield. The story surrounding her murder is complicated and resulted in an inquiry into her care and death. Toni-Ann, a young girl in the care of Birmingham Social Services, was shot in London in 2003 for witnessing the murder of her father, Bertram Byfield, an alleged drug dealer. Her case indicates that social workers have to take seriously the implications of drug use or dealing amongst parents and check out parental drug use before making decisions about the risks encountered by leaving children in their care.

The drug abuse case below shows the complex interventions needed in contemporary societies where crossing borders adds further layers to helping a substance abuser.

Case study: The personal costs of addiction

Henry, an 18-year-old British citizen, went to a summer camp in the USA during the holidays before attending Cardiff University. He had worked hard at his A levels, had done well and wanted a break. At the camp, he met some young Americans who were into recreational drug use. Never having been involved in such activities in the UK, he had a go. They were 'larking about' one afternoon when a teenager who had not spoken to them before joined them. After a while, he drew out a white substance that he passed round for everyone to snort. After this, the group sneaked into the woods for more every afternoon. By the end of the month, Henry was highly addicted to crystal meth.

He decided not to go to university that autumn, but join his new-found friends wandering around the USA in a second-hand 'Hummer' for a year. They were driving too fast on a bendy logging road in northern California one sunny afternoon, high on a cocktail of drugs, when they rolled off the road, turned over several times and crashed into a tree. Henry, the sole survivor, was badly hurt with severe neck and back injuries. The promising future that had beckoned weeks before had been wiped out in seconds and he had to embark on the long painful road to recovery.

The social worker who saw him in hospital was very encouraging and coaxed Henry into not giving up when he felt he would rather be dead. She convinced him that his pain could be managed and that he could resume his studies as a disabled student when he had healed from his physical injuries and his emotional traumas. Henry was not driving the vehicle at the time, but guilt at being the only survivor affected his psychological state immensely. Adding to this was that he had caused long-term damage to his body by being a crystal meth user. His social worker helped him to focus his attention on repairing his relationship with his parents and cooperating with the different health professionals who would help him regain much of his physical and mental capacities. She also contacted a lawyer to assist him with the forthcoming court case for drug misuse and eventual return to the UK.

Social workers who support substance abusers have to acquire a considerable amount of contextual, medical and other knowledge to intervene effectively. A holistic approach to their needs is important. Social workers can smooth relationship-building, especially in the formation of social networks that can give people a feeling of being valued, appreciated and belonging to a wider circle of people. This is crucial for young drug users, who often feel isolated and unwanted by their families. Social workers can advocate for better treatment facilities to be sited locally.

Social workers often use the 'Cycle of Change' model that James Prochaska et al. (1992, 1994) developed to educate and empower drug users in rehabilitation endeavours and offer practical steps in reducing drug abuse. The model emphasizes drug users' choice over the behaviours they engage in and responsibility for the choices they make. These focus on identifying the triggers that encourage drug misuse, recognizing high-risk situations, developing relapse prevention strategies and positive self-talk.

Whilst Henry's case may indicate that social work support in drug abuse situations is clear-cut, it fudges debate on the effectiveness of mandatory treatments for those who abuse substances. Most professionals working in this field believe that the likelihood of compliance and transcending the physical problems associated with withdrawal is greater if drug users volunteer to be helped rather than being coerced by a court order. The differences in opinion over this issue may test partnerships between the statutory and voluntary sector workers and jeopardize their involvement in specific cases because statutory workers are required to comply with court directions. Another difficulty is the criminal justice system becoming a key player in an area of practice traditionally dominated by the voluntary sector.

Although the end goal – helping people turn away from abusing drugs – is shared, each sector has a different approach on how it is reached. Each has its own organizational ethos, working practices and relationships with drug users. Those who work for agencies in the criminal justice system are required to place greater priority on protecting the public and controlling drug users than are voluntary sector workers, whose major aim is to initiate personal change. They attempt to persuade drug users to change their habits and empower them in taking control of their lives as a way of ending drug misuse. These two sectors have different responsibilities in addressing issues of confidentiality, with those in the statutory sector being required to report breaches of orders as routine. Different obligations may create tensions amongst workers and force those in the voluntary sector into following statutory sector protocols, with a consequent loss of professional autonomy. Voluntary sector workers fear that this will damage the relationships that they can form with drug users in a context in which establishing good connections between the worker and drug user is important in initiating the personal change processes that help in coming off drugs.

These tensions are evident in work with prisoners. Prisons have surveillance regimes to keep drugs out of prison and catch those trying to smuggle them in. Their success in achieving this aim is limited as drugs are easier to obtain here than the authorities would like. The importance of treating offenders in prisons has led to the creation of specific rehabilitative services for these drug users. In the late 1990s, the prison service developed the Counselling, Assessment, Referral, Advice and Throughcare (CARAT) scheme to tackle drug use in prisons and provide individually tailored responses to offenders seeking to end their abuse of drugs. CARAT workers are now present in every prison in England and help offenders link to community drug services prior to release. A range of professionals – e.g., probation officers, counsellors, group workers, therapists, psychologists and psychiatrists – address their needs. Thus, there are more drug workers working in prison settings and more offenders using community drug services than was previously the case.

The development of drug services in communities in the UK has been a local affair, with local projects to meet local aims, objectives and needs.

The National Treatment Agency (NTA), formed in 2001, has shifted this emphasis a bit by providing national guidance and models of treatment to create better services. Its remit sits uneasily with the traditions of a voluntary drug services sector that questions the appropriateness of a 'one size fits all' approach to the complicated matters raised by drug misuse.

Conclusions

Substance misuse is a difficult area of practice. Drug users pose specific and complex problems for social workers to address, often in seriously under-resourced situations. They may be working with drug users in either a voluntary or court-mandated capacity. Powers of persuasion, non-judgementalism and empathy are important skills needed in this work, regardless of the source of referral. The complications associated with withdrawal may test their patience alongside that of drug users'.

The recreational use of drugs has brought its own problems to practice. In giving greater legitimacy to drug use, including that of hard drugs, it has drawn more people into the net of those using these substances and added pressure to over-stretched resources for those wishing to withdraw. Its spread into the professional classes means that some practitioners who intervene in the lives of those misusing drugs might themselves be recreational drug users. This may affect their judgement about what level of drug use is acceptable amongst people who access their services. This may pose particular and unacceptable risks to children. Addressing the social circumstances, including the relationships that people experience, are crucial to finding successful solutions to the problem. Responding to drug misuse challenges politicians, social workers, other professionals and society alike. They must work effectively together to promote reductions in the misuse of substances ranging from hard drugs to alcohol.

8

Offending Behaviour and Working with Offenders

Rehabilitation or Warehousing?

Work with offenders has been the remit of a particular type of social worker – probation officers, who have straddled the contradiction between rehabilitating offenders or just 'warehousing' them as part of a strategy of keeping them out of trouble and 'protecting the public'. Working with offenders has traditionally been part of the social work remit. While this link continues in many countries, including Scotland, in England and Wales Jack Straw broke this connection in 1998, while retaining the link with social work for young offenders. Social workers and probation officers in the latter two countries no longer train alongside each other.

Probation officers work with other professionals in the criminal justice system, psychologists, psychiatrists and those in community and custodial settings. Most are community-based, but probation officers in prisons link communities with correctional institutions. Their location changes the nature of their relationship with inmates and other professionals. In the USA, probation officers have become correctional officers, indicating a more than symbolic shift from rehabilitating offenders to warehousing them in facilities owned by a private sector that profits from containing people convicted of offences. Private prisons have now also been established in the UK (HMPS, 2007).

Prison populations in the UK and the USA have reached historic heights: 120 and 800 per 100,000, respectively. Probation officers often challenge the use of prisons simply to 'warehouse' people and highlight the many untried or alleged offenders in areas like domestic violence and child sexual abuse. The large number of unreported and unconvicted violent offenders is seldom addressed but is cause for concern. 'Race' and racism are big issues in American penal services as the majority of those in prison and 'death row' are African American or 'black'. The over-representation of black people in prison statistics is also evident in Britain. The experiences of prison vary according to type of offender and personal attributes. Women, black people and mentally disordered offenders are most likely to receive the harshest sentences and most inappropriate forms of treatment. Crime rates are rising faster amongst women than men – 11 per cent to 6 per cent, respectively, in 2002. Black men are eight times more likely to be arrested than are white men. Black men are also four times more likely to be stopped, searched and released without charge than are white men.

In this chapter, I consider difficulties in working with offenders in contexts of limited resources and the over-riding preoccupation of professionals to control rather than change behaviours or lifestyles of convicted people. Thus, I argue for a strong rehabilitative element in social work practice that is undertaken with offenders.

Working with Offenders: Control, Care and Befriending in Probation Practice

Working with offenders is divided into adult services and those for young offenders. The age of criminal responsibility in the UK is 10, much lower than in many other European countries. On the continent, 15 or 18 years of age is deemed the lowest acceptable age. In Britain, young people are sent to young offender institutions to serve their sentences. This does not mean that the regime is any less severe than in adult prisons, though young offenders are more likely than adult offenders to receive some educational input.

Prison numbers are at full capacity. In the early 1990s Roger Graef (1992) revealed that one in three British men under 30 had been convicted of a non-motoring offence. This figure has increased since then, and the numbers of people (mainly men) in British prisons have reached an all-time high of over 80,000 by 2006 – double the numbers when Graef wrote. Most crime is committed by a limited number of persistent offenders: 100,000 adults and 3,000 juveniles. These statistics raise questions about the kind of society being created if a high proportion of citizens are criminalized and existing custodial institutions are seriously overcrowded.

The public perceives crime statistics as rising, regardless of government figures. It fears becoming victims of crime on the streets and at home, even without considering the most recent terrorist threat to public security. Public support for a rehabilitative approach to offenders is dwindling. The growth of surveillance technology like CCTV, speed cameras and tagging offenders is now commonplace. These developments are rarely debated for their impact on civil liberties. Moreover, surveillance and technological controls have become racialized, with black men being subjected to them more than white men: 37 per cent of recorded DNA is of black men. This is a proportion of an increasingly large total. In 2007, 547,020 DNA samples were added to the police database – about an entry a minute.

The probation service was formed out of the nineteenth-century Missionary Courts, which originally focused on white adult men offenders. These had the police acting as probation officers who assisted and befriended offenders in the hopes of encouraging them to change and adopt socially acceptable norms in their conduct. This approach has become highly contentious because the causes of crime and what constitute the best responses to convicted offenders are disputed. Probation officers today are expected to protect the public and prevent re-offending (recidivism). Although contested, the incorporation of the National Probation Service and Prison Service in the National Offender Management Service (NOMS) in 2004 signalled the shift to greater central control of probation, increased workloads, less time for welfare-based interventions and a market in offender-related services (Carter, 2003; NOMS, 2006). The Offender Management Act 2007 proposed the creation of probation trusts. Probation areas not reaching trust status by 2010 could find their services opened up to other providers or trusts.

NOMS promotes an Offender Management Model for adults with community sentences. According to this model, an offender manager, case administrator, key worker and offender supervisor aim to 'punish, help, change and control' offenders and their behaviour (Knott, 2006: 49). Probation officers have successfully contained some offending behaviour while problems remain in certain areas. The tendency of ex-offenders to re-offend or commit further crimes increases the longer the period after completion of a sentence. Those who serve custodial sentences fare no better – 70 to 80 per cent of ex-offenders re-offend within two years of leaving prison.

The threat of prison to ensure compliance with social norms has been a fundamental dimension of the controlling aspects of prison regimes and probation. Enforcing compliance to social norms constitutes what Michel Foucault (1991) referred to as 'disciplining' people through self-imposed forms of obedience. Prisons were, according to him, key sites in which the state's attempts to ensure that people controlled their own behaviour proved instructive in how to control those outside their walls. Prisoners have also been used as cheap labour, leading some to argue that this 'reserve army of labour' is used to depress wage levels for other workers. Zygmunt Bauman (2000) has recently challenged this thesis. Deeming it no longer necessary, he argues that the warehousing function is more prominent. By warehousing, he means keeping those who do not behave in accordance with social norms in institutions that are not concerned with their rehabilitation or education for the purposes of getting a job. This approach suits the owners of private prisons, who reduce staff salaries and educational provisions to maximize profits. Private firms downplay rehabilitative work with offenders. Warehousing seems sufficient in relating to them. Prisoners have challenged being warehoused. In the 1990s, sex offenders in Kingston Prison, Canada, took the federal government to court for not providing training and other resources for their rehabilitation and reintegration into their communities. They claimed that simply warehousing them without concern for their welfare post-release was a violation of their human rights. In the UK, ex-offenders have founded organizations that have demanded the abolition of prisons. Their claims merit serious consideration.

The British government's unwillingness to fund public prisons has encouraged the growth of private ones – an outcome once considered unethical on the grounds that it was immoral to profit from crime. This injunction seems limited largely to offenders or ex-offenders, who are prevented from receiving large sums of money for writing stories about either their crimes or treatment whilst serving their sentences. Some find a way of doing so, e.g., Jeffrey Archer. The UK has 11 private prisons run by multi-national firms. Four secure training centres (STCs) for young offenders are privately run under Home Office contract. Companies running private prisons also run immigration detention centres. Yarl's Wood in Oxfordshire was set on fire by those detained in protest at their poor treatment. The damage was so severe that its insurers threatened to withdraw cover from similar institutions (Goodchild, 2002).

Probation officers objected to private prisons through the National Association of Probation Officers (NAPO, now the Trade Union and Professional Association for Family Court and Probation Staff) on the grounds that profiting from containing offenders is inappropriate and betrays public sensitivities. New Labour is disinclined to address these concerns, viewing the need to save public funds a greater priority. Whether this will be the case in the long run is disputed, not least because the Private Finance Initiative (PFI) and public–private partnerships (PPPs) responsible for the construction of private custodial facilities involve financing arrangements that privilege the private sector through favourable subsidies and taxation. In addition, private prisons are associated with repayment schemes that stretch into the distant future to create a public debt burden that might become both a financial and a political liability.

Policy became a driving factor behind changes in professional practice and introduced 'new' managerialist practices to hold probation officers accountable for their work. This covered stipulations about the frequency of supervising and processing offenders that were incorporated into National Standards. This approach deviated from the 'economics as ideology' approach to changing professional behaviour favoured by Tory administrations in the 1990s. Under this, budgetary allocations controlled professional activities by driving what could be purchased, the conditions of sale, for whom and from which organization, e.g., requiring 5 per cent of probation budgets to be spent procuring provisions from voluntary agencies (Knott, 2006). Under New Labour, the 1998 Crime and Disorder Act brought partnership working into the probation service and endorsed populist top-down perspectives in managing crime. This affirmed probation officers' role in safeguarding communities by preventing offending.

Risk Assessment and Management

Risk assessment and risk management are central to the 'new managerialism' in the probation service. Risk management systems enable managers to: exercise greater bureaucratic control over workers; know more effectively what they are doing when working with offenders; and evaluate the impact of interventions. Risk management has benefits the public can see and accounts for how professionals disburse time and resources. However, it removes professional judgement from many interventions, including those where purely bureaucratic responses are counter-productive. Under risk management regimes, a probation officer calculates the risk of harm that each offender poses to him/herself and the public. Probation officers, psychiatrists and psychologists use knowledge accumulated through risk assessment instruments to control dangerous individuals. Their approach can give the public a false sense of security because risk assessments are not wholly scientific or reliable in predicting dangerous behaviour, especially amongst mentally disordered offenders (Quinsey, 1995). Risk management aims to manage crime, not to address its causes or reduce it.

Victimology

The criminal justice system has been criticized for not taking seriously the views of victims and for siding with offenders. Feminist social workers, probation officers and criminologists have hammered this message home, especially in work on domestic violence and sexual abuse. They have highlighted the social construction of masculinity as crucial to handling violent men convicted of these offences. They have also initiated important innovations in practice with violent men and encouraged male probation officers to work with them from perspectives sympathetic to feminist objectives (Wild, 1999).

These endeavours eventually gave rise to the study of victimology to take on board victim's interests, particularly in those areas where women were the main victims of male crimes, as in domestic violence and sexual abuse. The Victims' Charters initiated by John Major as Prime Minister aimed to improve the relationship between victims and professionals working in the criminal justice system. A study conducted by Jackie Tapley (2002) at Southampton University found that these initiatives had not ended the exclusion of victims' perspectives from the criminal justice system's handling of offenders. A telling example of this failure was the exposure of probation officers' inability to alert victims about the pending release of offenders who had victimized them. In one instance, a woman found out about the release of her attacker by meeting him on the High Street!

Increasing demands for victims' voices to be included in what happens to offenders has yielded new responses to young offenders. These include restorative justice, which balances the interests of both offenders and victims. Restorative justice with young offenders in the UK had a major boost in the 1990s with the development of Family Group Conferences (FGCs), a system adapted from New Zealand/Aotearoa. FGCs are based on the Maori philosophy of diverting young people from custody by retaining them in their communities and involving their extended family in planning for their rehabilitation as useful members of the community.

Differentiated Justice for Different Categories of Offenders

Offenders are a diverse group. Its constituents experience the criminal justice system differently. This can be construed as differentiated justice and includes women, black offenders, disabled offenders and mentally disordered offenders. White women offenders are considered less dangerous than white men offenders because they are imprisoned primarily for prostitution-related offences like soliciting and shoplifting if they have not paid their fines. Black women offenders are considered 'dangerous' and more likely to get custodial sentences than are white women offenders. Women first-time offenders are more likely to be imprisoned than are men (Fawcett Society, 2007).

Class is another significant basis of differentiation, with the policing of working-class communities, black and white, being higher than that of middle-class ones (Young, 1999). Working-class offenders tend to commit crime within their own communities to raise income or finance drug habits. Wealthy people can afford to buy surveillance equipment that deters burglars from entering their premises. They can also pay top lawyers, who have a better chance of successfully arguing their case for not being 'sent down'; working-class people cannot. This leads to accusations of one law for rich and another for poor people. This is particularly evident in the limited prosecutions of executives involved in fraud or otherwise misusing funds at their disposal. Enron and Conrad Black provide recent rare examples. The inaccessibility of justice for poor people is being exacerbated as British legal aid is withdrawn from situations where it previously applied. Attempts to curtail overall legal aid costs have caused lawyers to reduce services and jeopardized free advice centres, some employing social workers.

Black offenders are disproportionately imprisoned and seen as dangerous or violent in the public imagination: 1 in 100 black adult men in Britain is in prison. The image of black men as violent is fanned by media coverage of their involvement in offending behaviour, including a recent spate of shootings. Violence, the use of guns and failure of police to respond appropriately to the murder of black teenagers has worried black communities for some time. The most infamous cases of police inaction concerned the murder of young black men by young white men, as occurred to Stephen Lawrence in London in 1993 and Anthony Walker in Liverpool in 2005. The Macpherson (1999) Report into Stephen's murder criticized police inaction, called it *institutional racism* and demanded crucial changes in how the police addressed these offences. These included 'freedom of information' for the public to hold police accountable for their actions and more rights for victims in racist incidents. Macpherson defined a racist incident as one considered such by victims.

Sustained attempts to reduce racism in the probation service date back to the 1980s. These cover: becoming aware of the impact of racist attitudes in practice, especially those relating to the types of services available to black offenders; writing reports for court; and black people's employment in the service. Despite these initiatives, a report written in 2000 claimed that racism continued to feature in probation practice. In it, Chief Inspector of Probation, Sir Graham Smith, found that white officers felt uncomfortable writing pre-sentence inquiry reports on black offenders and did not make recommendations about an appropriate sentence. Thus, black offenders had harsher sentences: 15 per cent of the prison population was black. Black people fared no better as potential employees. None of the 54 chief probation officers was black, and only a handful of the 200 associate chief probation officers were black (CJB, 2007). This was despite the formation in 1982 and 1987, respectively, of the Association of Black Probation Officers and the National Association of Asian Probation Staff to promote their interests.

Young Offenders

Young offenders in their teen years are responsible for 40 per cent of burglaries and 28 per cent of violent offences in the UK (Lyon et al., 2000). Young offenders in custody can be placed in young offenders' institutions (YOIs), secure training units (STUs), secure children's homes and secure training centres (STCs). The law and order debates concerning very young offenders revolve around whether to provide for their welfare or secure justice for victims. These constituted the welfare–justice debates conducted primarily in the juvenile justice part of the probation service during the 1980s. The former focuses on young offenders having opportunities to change and move away from careers in crime. The justice approach is concerned primarily with punishment and protecting the public from harm. The tension between welfare and justice in youth offending has a long history. The high point of welfare over justice as the over-riding concern in work with young offenders was the 1969 Children and Young Persons Act. This allowed for intermediate treatment (IT), whereby probation officers and social workers stressed rehabilitation and integration of young offenders in communities. IT projects stressed outdoor activities and outreach to foster personal growth. Widespread use of IT ended in the 1980s when justice superseded welfare as the key principle in work with young offenders. Policy now focuses on appropriate punishment for offenders and protecting the public, including victims of crime. This can bring the goals in working with adult and young offenders closer together.

Justice-based interventions are fuelled by media hysteria and authoritarian politicians riding a populist wave to power. Following the murder of the toddler James Bulger in 1993 by two 10-year-old boys, young offenders, may of whom have ended up offending for multiple reasons often not of their making, have found themselves increasingly de-humanized in the media with epithets such as 'Feral Child' and 'Rat Boy'. 'Rat Boy', a classic example of a troubled young man who survived through crime, burgled homes in Tyneside and lived in heating ducts, hence the name (Raymond, 2007). 'Safari Boy' was the epithet given to a young offender in Gloucester because his probation officer sent him on safari to build his character as part of a behavioural change strategy under the IT model.

Demonizing young people was an expression of the popularization of applying the 'short, sharp shock' to custodial sentencing and changing behaviour. The tough regimes favoured by Conservative Home Secretary Michael Howard had a limited impact on reducing offending, and programmes to divert young people from incarceration co-existed alongside the detention centres he endorsed. Commentators argue that his predecessor, Douglas Hurd, had enlightened responses to young offenders in the early 1990s. Conditional discharge and intensive supervision enjoyed court confidence. Police cautions were an extremely effective intervention strategy: 80 per cent of those so warned never appeared before the courts and crime amongst young offenders did not increase. Hurd's approach of low tariff sentences with targeted intensive supervision was accompanied by low rates of custodial sentencing and highlights the impact of public policy on crime statistics.

Work with young offenders had achieved successes before New Labour replaced the previous juvenile justice system with the Youth Justice Board (YJB) and swapped a professionally orientated approach for a managerialist one favoured by techno-bureaucrats. Social workers and probation officers who worked with young offenders rarely conducted research on the effectiveness of their practice. Keith Haines (2002) suggests this underpins New Labour's failure to appreciate earlier successes with young offenders. Without proof, New Labour could ignore them and focus on greater administrative accountability and control over their practice when it assumed power. The YJB and Youth Offending Teams (YOTs) created as part of the Youth Justice System (YJS) under Section 37 of the 1998 Crime and Disorder Act became responsible for young offenders. The YJB monitors the activities of YOTs, is charged with formulating a local crime reduction and community safety plan, and oversees its implementation by working in partnership with other agencies to protect communities from criminals.

YOTs work with young offenders serving sentences in the community. They are multi-professional teams composed of social workers, probation officers, the police, teachers, psychologists and other professionals working together to support young offenders and promote the outcomes of *Every Child Matters*. YOTs' key purposes are to keep young people out of trouble, prevent re-offending, protect the public and reduce fear of crime. These drive New Labour's endeavours in this area and intensify its preoccupation with controlling both young offenders and professionals working with them. YOTs emphasize punishment and restitution more than Intermediate Treatment Teams did, but engage in some innovative initiatives: for example, the project InSide/Out has offenders restoring the Monastery of St Francis in Gorton, Greater Manchester, on the grounds that such sentences are more effective than custody.

Government holds YOTs accountable with a managerialist overview of performance measures based on YJB plans, and it endorses a top-down approach to youth justice that reduces the space in which practitioners can exercise cautious professional judgement in responding to young offenders. YOTs process a child through: a final warning; recommending referral orders; running youth offender panels; completing ASSET assessments, i.e., structured assessments of risks and protective factors that affect offending behaviour; and supervising offenders after release from custody. How they carry out these tasks depends on the philosophy of YOT workers. They can follow a mechanistic, top-down approach linked to national standards or adapt these to local conditions and individual offenders. YOTs can subvert administrative procedures that merely implement government policy by doing what in their professional opinion is best for a particular child. YOTs and Family Group Conferences have replaced the 'boot camps' that Michael Howard endorsed as Home Secretary.

Local authorities are responsible for maintaining secure units for young offenders. There are 445 approved places in secure units in England and Wales. Around 42 per cent of those in 'secure accommodation' are on Detention and Training Orders (DTOs). With these, the courts signal the intention that young people receive education and training to prepare them for a better life when they leave these facilities. Of those placed in them, 18 per cent are black and 32 per cent are women, indicating that both groups are over-represented (ONS, 2001). These operate largely on a one-size-fits-all basis; both sexes are placed in them. Scotland's first secure unit for girls, the Good Shepherd Centre in Bishopton, opened in 2006. Private secure training centres (STCs) provide education and rehabilitation services. There are four in England.

The current drive in the probation service in England and Wales has been towards specialist and targeted programmes. These belie a normalization approach that reintegrates offenders into their communities and addresses an offender's needs as a whole person. 'Evidence-based practice' (EBP) is used to identify 'what works' with offenders and aims to reduce recidivism rates or likelihood of re-offending. EBP has become a buzzword in probation circles. Cognitive-behavioural programmes and accreditation of staff able to undertake such activities have endorsed offender-orientated and offence-focused activities over community-based ones. The latter approach can be effective with young people if it encourages them to engage in meaningful day-time pursuits. However, 70 to 80 per cent of those currently on supervision orders have not been integrated into such endeavours. If these opportunities had been presented to them, they could go some way towards introducing meaning and order into otherwise chaotic lives that thrive on alcohol, drugs and further offending. It could also reduce their feelings of alienation and social exclusion from wider society.

Social workers can use provisions in international conventions to enhance IT objectives and work with young offenders in their communities. The United Nations Convention on the Rights of the Child (CRC) 1989, to which the UK is a signatory, criticized the way in which the British criminal justice system treats young offenders. The CRC defines a child as anyone under 18. The UN Standard Minimum Rules for the Administration of Juvenile Justice, or 'Beijing Rules', of 1985 state that juvenile justice should operate within a framework of the 'best interests' of the young offender who is treated as a child. This injunction echoes Article 3 of the CRC. The interpretation of the term 'best interests of the child' is a contentious one, although the CRC presumes that items constituting a normal life are covered, with education, health and leisure activities specifically mentioned. However, the Beijing Rules are not legally binding in the way that the CRC is.

Controlling Civil and Criminal Behaviour through Authoritarian Populism and Anti-Social Behaviour Orders

Authoritarian populism involves politicians conducting 'law and order' debates in punitive terms because they think it appeals to the masses. Both New Labour and the Conservatives have employed this approach to stem the loss of public confidence in a criminal justice system that no longer seems fit for purpose given the perceived increases in crime rates over the years. The system's emphasis on public confidence and attempts to control offending behaviour has blurred the boundaries between criminal behaviour that resulted in custodial sentences and civil action that did not.

The emphasis on community safety and creating civility within local spaces has led to the creation of Anti-Social Behaviour Orders (ASBOs) under New Labour. ASBOs have been used to curb a variety of behaviours, including truancy and those who have violated parenting orders. They were originally designed as a civil measure, but failure to observe conditions attached to ASBOs has resulted in many young people being breached for non-compliance and receiving a prison sentence for an 'offence' that initially was not a criminal act. The breaching or taking to court of those who do not comply with the conditions of their ASBOs means that people who violate civil norms may end up in prison.

ASBOs have been symptomatic of New Labour's 'zero tolerance' approach to young offenders. Its determination to punish rather than rehabilitate young people can be construed as anti-child. This is likely to be a short-sighted policy undermining years of successful interventions that kept young people out of a prison system that made bad criminals even worse. The success of ASBOs in controlling unruly behaviour has been challenged. There is considerable unease that they are being used inappropriately to punish people with behaviour that is objectionable but not criminal, e.g., rowdy playing on the streets and using foul language, alongside more serious activities involving bullying and assault. ASBOs are disproportionately used to control young people's behaviour, but have covered people in their 70s and 80s too.

ASBOs have criminalized a widening range of behaviours and reflect the growth in authoritarian populism perpetrated in and through the state. This has criminalized people whose misdeeds would be better addressed by other means. The story of Patricia Amos, imprisoned because her children truanted, is instructive in this respect.

Case study: Holding parents accountable for their children's behaviour

Patricia Amos, a single mother from Banbury, was imprisoned for 60 days for not ensuring that her children attended school in 2002. This was reduced to 28 days upon appeal, and she spent 14 days in Holloway Prison for women. Despite promises of having learnt from her experiences and her daughters returning to school, Patricia was sentenced to a further 28 days in 2004 when she proved unable to prevent one of them from truanting again. The mother's problems with drug misuse and low income that had initially worried her daughters sufficiently to cause them to stay home from school to look after her were inadequately addressed and continued to impede the development of new options in life. Thus, it is not surprising that Patricia returned to her previous behaviour once back at home and ended up before the courts anew.

Individualizing Approaches to Offending Behaviour

Cognitive-behavioural therapy (CBT) is used widely in social work interventions. It aims to change a person's behaviour by examining how cognition affects conduct and drawing connections between actions and their consequences. It is popular in work with offenders because it quantifies individual offending behaviour and impact. CBT is effective insofar as it holds individual offenders responsible for their actions. It fails, however, to address inequalities and the structural underpinnings of offending behaviour like poverty, loss of status, place in society and the role of masculinity in crime. Masculinity legitimates men's position as powerful social actors, and endorses their aggressive behaviour and their expectations that other people will do their bidding (Pringle, 1995). Behaviour predicated upon this view of masculinity is suited to CBT-based interventions.

CBT draws on: *antecedents* (A) – the circumstances in which behaviour takes place; *behaviour* (B) – what the person actually does; and *consequences* (C) – what happens immediately after the behaviour occurs (Cigno, 2002: 186). Known as the ABC of CBT-based interventions, this approach is often used by probation officers working with violent offenders, especially adult ones who sexually abuse children. It alters behaviour by better understanding its causes and consequences. It also gives a people confidence in their ability to do things differently under their own steam. Offenders have to take responsibility for what they have done and what they are going to do to change. CBT encourages men sex offenders to address power relations linked to expectations about masculinity in their relationships with women and children. It also requires them to consider their relationships with other men as these can encourage 'power over' relationships that result in their abusing people in subordinate positions.

CBT interventions are not always reliable: foe example, a sex offender can think his behaviour has changed when it has not. Sex offenders can assert that they have changed, but failure to empathize with victims makes them reject this claim. Victims can show that offenders have learnt the jargon instead of changing their behaviour and understanding. This is evidenced in instances of restorative justice when an offender who has sought to change is faced by a victim-survivor who labels that change 'superficial'. This failure is demonstrated by John, a violent offender, who physically assaulted his wife.

Case study: Superficial changes in an offender's behaviour and understanding

John was a 30-year-old man of white British descent who had a lengthy history of fighting with other men. After serving time, he met Sally, five years younger than him. Her impact on him was profound and he believed that she had turned his life around. He had not beaten men up for some time, although he continued to drink heavily. Sally and John were married and seemed happy for their first year together. Shortly after their anniversary, John lost his job as a driver and began to hit Sally on the slightest pretext. He carried on physically abusing her despite promising to change. Sally thought about how to deal with the issue, but as he was contrite after each episode, she kept giving him another chance. She kept quiet about it so as not to embarrass her parents and his family. She did not want to admit that her mother's reservations about her marriage were better founded than her optimism. John beat her up so savagely one night she needed hospital treatment. The police, called by neighbours who heard her screams, got Sally to prosecute for assault. John received a 12-month custodial sentence for grievous bodily harm. Whilst in prison, his probation officer suggested he join anger management classes and a group for violent men. This he did, feeling he understood his behaviour and could control his temper better.

Sally did not visit him in prison and had mixed views about whether he should return home or whether she should seek an injunction and divorce. In the end, she agreed he could come back for a trial period. She was cooking dinner one evening when she dropped the casserole containing a stew she was making and it smashed on the floor. John, who rushed through to the kitchen on hearing the noise, started calling her names for being so sloppy and could feel his temper rising. He suddenly shouted 'Time Out!' at the top of his voice and rushed out of the room before a startled and frightened Sally could say a word. He returned two hours later, having been to the pub for supper without ringing to tell her.

Sally was distraught at this behaviour. When she began to explain why she felt as she did, John shouted her down, calling her names again and ending with, 'I had to leave. Otherwise, I would have thumped you for wasting my dinner. See, that's how much I've changed.' Sally realized then that John's behaviour would never change so that he would truly respect her and do his share of household chores. She decided they could not remain together and resolved to leave, happy that there were no children to complicate the picture.

John portrays a man who has learnt the jargon in the CBT and anger management sessions he attended, but not their substance. He cannot see the disrespectful way he reacts to Sally or acknowledge that the world revolves around his needs, to the total disregard of hers. He uses his knowledge of techniques to control situations and dominate Sally rather than work with her to their mutual satisfaction.

Conclusions

Work with offenders is an important, if fraught, part of social work. The link between probation and social work has been severed recently in England and Wales except for young offenders. Experiences of the criminal justice system vary according to class, 'race' and gender, with black men and women offenders receiving harsher treatment than their white counterparts. Probation practice has been criticized in the same way as social work practice more generally for failing to keep its charges in check. Under the imperative of reducing offending and protecting the public, government has given less attention to the welfare needs of offenders. Work with them has become individualized and incapable of linking individual offending behaviour to the social relations in which a person is embedded.

Professional disquiet about a system that is failing stakeholders, rising levels of crime and overcrowding in prisons indicates failure in current approaches to offending. The present emphasis on punishment without rehabilitation is unsustainable in the long run. Probation officers can bring the inadequacies of the criminal justice system to public notice and ensure that work with offenders resumes its rightful priority of rehabilitation in accordance with social work values. Training can reinforce these elements by highlighting research that compares the benefits to communities of rehabilitating offenders with those of warehousing them.

9

Disaster Interventions

Immediate Relief or Long-Term Reconstruction?

Disasters can be caused by both nature and human beings. Their intensity and frequency of occurrence seem to be increasing. Some observers argue that this is caused by global warming creating serious imbalances in environmental conditions. Others contend that it is because industrial processes have gone out of control as regulations governing company behaviour have been ignored. Individual activists like Vandana Shiva and Arundhati Roy in India and groups like Greenpeace in the West are taking environmental destruction seriously to protest against large-scale infrastructural ventures like building large dams that can trigger disasters. Such projects displace substantial numbers of poor people whose meagre resources are strained without adequate compensation. Terrorism and armed conflicts exacerbate fragile situations, adding further pollution and misery by exploding bombs, burning oil and mining inhabited land.

Social workers are amongst professionals who intervene in disaster situations, whether caused by people or nature. They assist in the immediate aftermath and during long-term reconstruction. There is a long history of social workers acting in disasters, e.g., those covering floods, droughts, mudslides and armed conflicts in poor industrializing countries. Many of these endeavours, especially in poor African countries like Mozambique, Ethiopia and Somalia, involve international voluntary organizations, such as the Red Cross and Oxfam, that provide immediate relief in the event of a disaster. Hurricane Dean, a Category 5 hurricane and one of most intense since records began in the 1850s, ravaged the Caribbean and Yucatán Peninsula in Mexico from 19 to 22 August 2007. It killed 22 people, ruined many poor people's homes and forced oil rigs in Mexico's Cantarell oil field – the third largest in the world – to be shut down and 19,000 workers evacuated. Social workers, including those linked to World Vision Mexico, helped people into pre-arranged shelters before the storm and to cope with the aftermath afterwards.

The 26 December 2004 tsunami that devastated people in 12 nations bordering the Indian Ocean was amongst the largest natural disasters of modern times (see case study on p. 147). Poor countries like Indonesia bore the brunt of the tsunami and the earthquake that preceded it, with horrendous loss of life and property. This calamity may be dwarfed by damage caused by Cyclone Nargis in Myanmar/Burma during May 2008, where military rulers refused international aid for the first three weeks following. In contrast, and despite large-scale need and the vast numbers affected, the state in China responded with commendable efficiency following the severe earthquakes, aftershocks and flooding in Sichuan province that same month, using the army to rescue people and bury the dead while social workers fed, housed and emotionally supported survivors. Recent disasters have also occurred in the industrialized West. Social workers have relieved trauma and suffering after: the attack on the World Trade Center in New York on 11 September 2001; the bombings on trains in Madrid on 11 March 2004; the London Underground bombings on 7 July 2005; the destruction wrought by Hurricane Katrina in New Orleans on 2 September 2005; and the floods in the UK in 2007.

Social workers' roles in disaster situations are many and diverse. They include that of:

- facilitator;
- coordinator;
- community mobilizer (of people and systems);
- mobilizer of resources;
- negotiator or broker between communities and different levels of government;
- mediator between conflicting interests and groups;
- consultant to government and other agencies;
- advocate for people's rights and entitlements;
- educator, giving out information about how to access relief aid and avoid diseases that can erupt following a disaster; and

- therapist, helping people deal with the emotional consequences of disaster.

Disaster relief is big business. It involves public, private and voluntary organizations that employ half a million people globally and disburse more than 60 million euros. The potential for abuse in disaster relief operations and for misappropriation of substantial sums is considerable. This includes: institutionalized forms like tying aid to national priorities, e.g., the USA insisting 70 per cent of promised disaster funds is spent in America; giving inappropriate items like electric domestic refrigerators for houses that lack electricity; and corruption and greed amongst those distributing aid.

John Pilger (2005) adds that aid places industrializing countries in a dependency relationship vis-à-vis rich ones, and this is itself a disaster. He suggests that the way that aid is distributed encourages dependency and deprives local people of the right to make their own decisions. It also thwarts their primary reliance on local resources, thereby leaving donated ones to assume a more than supplementary role. Fear of local development becoming subordinated to foreign interventions convinced the Indian government to refuse relief aid during the tsunami. But it gave aid to other countries. This act of seeming generosity was criticized because there was not enough aid to deal with India's own problems. Cynics suggested that the Indian government gave to ensure it acquires superpower status in the region. Social workers have to be aware of such complexities in disaster arenas as these conditions may limit what they can do.

Social work interventions in disaster situations are complex. They may require political commitment from government(s) to make this work possible. Aid collected through diverse agencies from many countries requires skilful organization to be distributed in areas where the basic service infrastructure may have collapsed (if it existed initially). It calls on forms of solidarity that cross many types of borders – geographical, religious and cultural; it demands practice skills capable of delivering a sophisticated blend of services; it covers the emotional, physical, economic and social needs of those seeking to rebuild their lives; and it requires empowering values.

In this chapter, I consider social work interventions in the immediate aftermath of disasters and longer-term reconstruction to examine the roles social workers occupy alongside other professionals and people living in the affected areas. Human rights and social justice are crucial to these endeavours and indicate the importance of social work as a professional activity that builds on existing skills and resources as it brings new ones into an area to assist in long-term reconstruction. I explore the changes in social arrangements that such interventions create from the perspective of those involved. As often occurs in complex situations, there are both pluses and minuses to be weighed in evaluating the outcomes of social work action in them. A seldom talked-about negative aspect of this work is the dangers that social workers run.

Social Work Interventions in Disaster Situations

Social workers in disaster situations intervene in multi-disciplinary teams alongside other professionals. Their work is often taken for granted in that it addresses the everyday needs of people affected by disasters and rarely receives the limelight in newspaper coverage of disaster situations. Social workers are mainly involved in assessing needs that have to be met in both the short and long term. They are also expected to find resources to meet these needs. This can require social workers to engage with policymakers to secure the necessaries and can call upon political skills alongside communication ones. Even so, resources are rarely adequate for the needs of the people affected and social workers may require help in addressing the negative impact on their own psychic health of failure to meet need.

Disaster relief workers, including social workers, can find their own lives at risk. They may be taken hostage, raped (especially women) or even killed. A recent high-profile case involved the murder of 22 United Nations personnel, including their envoy, Sergio Vieira de Mello, when their Baghdad Headquarters were bombed in August 2003, causing the UN to pull out foreign staff. Few overseas relief workers had returned by August 2007, although the United States and Britain were arguing for the UN to play a greater role in Iraq given the civil war and chaos reigning in the country.

Intervening in disaster situations can be very complex work that involves many different players, each playing different roles. But as the case study below of developments in a recent Peruvian earthquake indicates, help is neither easy to get to affected regions nor distributed equitably when it arrives. This can increase survivors' sense of vulnerability, and as the people of Pisco demonstrated, they can act in an unhelpful manner, as they take matters into their own hands to speed up the aid distribution process. In doing so, such initiatives can jeopardize the chances of others to survive as much-needed assistance fails to reach them.

Case study: Disaster situations require complex interventions and many skills

On 15 August 2007, an earthquake with its epicentre 200 kilometres south of Lima and measuring 8.0 on the Richter Scale devastated large parts of Peru. It killed at least 540 people, injuring hundreds of others and left from 60,000 to 200,000 homeless. The total numbers are unknown as many of the affected villages are difficult to reach; many are without communications links to the outer world; and bodies lie buried under mountains of rubble. Poor people were disproportionately affected because their adobe houses crumbled in the earthquake and its aftermath. The quake was followed by 300 aftershocks which aggravated the situation and extended damage to a wider area. Lack of coordination, high levels of damage and poor transportation infrastructure in parts of Peru delayed the arrival of aid and skilled personnel to coordinate the delivery of supplies and ensure an equitable distribution of relief. Residents blocked the highway near Pisco where an air force base was used to centralize the delivery of airlifted supplies, and they commandeered and raided trucks carrying aid to different locations, including Ica, the provincial capital.

Pisco, a coastal town of 130,000, was one of the worst hit and 'looked like it had been bombed' – 85 per cent of its housing was lost and the port was damaged. Water and electricity supplies were disrupted. A church collapsed, trapping hundreds of mourners attending a funeral service inside. Tents, food, water and medicine were in short supply. Families took shelter in constructions made of cardboard and blankets held up by wooden poles. These were of limited use as temperatures dropped precipitously at night. Burial plots were scarce because huge numbers had died. Over 1,200 armed soldiers patrolled the streets to prevent looting. The massive level of destruction and harsh conditions meant that between 30 and 40 per cent of Pisco's citizens became refugees outside the devastated area.

In Chincha, another badly hit town, 600 prisoners escaped when the walls of the local prison tumbled down. Communication channels and transportation routes were so disrupted that officials could not tell 2,000 people who gathered in the town square when help would reach them. The situation was so bad that Peru's President, Alan Garcia, took direct control of aid operations. Difficult situations like these can arise even where local social workers, trained in disaster relief interventions, are available to bring order to the chaos, help allay people's fears and distribute aid equitably. There are never enough local social workers to respond to the immense needs that overwhelm people. International social work organizations provide aid in these situations and acquire a great deal of expertise that should be passed on to local agencies. (Munoz, 2007: A14)

Immediate disaster responses involve social workers in: providing medical supplies, food and accommodation; linking survivors with relatives, friends and other survivors; and helping people deal with those who are missing, presumed dead or dead. Social workers are crucial in counselling people to help survive disaster, to allay feelings of guilt in being lucky enough to have escaped, or to deal with grief in losing loved ones. Long-term reconstruction absorbs social workers in community-based initiatives to restore infrastructure like housing, roads, communication networks, power-lines, hospitals, medical clinics, schools and economic activities. They also act as coordinators across several sectors, organizations and levels of government. In Pisco, this involved supporting complex initiatives, including rebuilding the port, the fishermen's wharf and associated facilities.

These situations produce large numbers of refugees who seek solace and safety outside the area. Their departure for safe havens can be a risky undertaking that may end in their deaths. This is instanced by Africans fleeing fighting in Sierra Leone who drowned at sea in flimsy boats drafted in for the purpose. Refugees may pay huge sums to individuals who promise to take them to safety. For some, it means years in exile without finances or material resources. This is more likely to happen to those escaping armed conflicts, e.g., the Palestinians who have been refugees in Jordan for more than 50 years. Their numbers may be more than a country can maintain without external support. This is the case for 2 million refugees from Iraq currently receiving succour in Jordan, where limited social work resources are severely overstretched. In other situations, individuals reach a safe country after a long and hazardous journey only to be refused entry and imprisoned, thus undergoing further trauma and abuse.

This is particularly relevant for women, because the 1951 Geneva Convention that defines the term 'refugee' excludes women's specific plight as refugees and treats them as if they encounter the same problems as men or denies the relevance of their different needs to their situation.

This happened to Fauziya Kassindja when, escaping the practice of female genital mutilation, she sought refugee status in the USA. Her lengthy struggle to be accepted as a refugee woman is poignantly detailed in *Do They Hear You When You Cry?* (Kassindja and Miller-Basher, 1998). Her groundbreaking struggle extended the meaning of the term 'refugee'. It now covers women's specific concerns linked to domestic violence, sexual assault and rape.

Social work educators in many countries train practitioners for intervention in disaster situations and use students in aid endeavours during such occasions. For example, the TATA Institute in India has an extensive history of involving students in helping victim-survivors in the immediate aftermath of disasters, including Bhopal (Desai, 2007; see also below); students in Iran rushed to aid people in the Bam earthquake of 2003 (Javadian, 2007); and social work students from Hong Kong assisted in disaster relief associated with the 2004 tsunami (Tang and Cheung, 2007). British students rarely cover this area in their curriculum, but severe flooding in Humberside, Warwickshire, Worcestershire and Yorkshire in the summer of 2007 suggests that they should.

These interventions require skills that draw heavily on: core social work values such as self-determination, equality, empowerment and justice; skills like interviewing and needs assessments; and organizational and communication skills. This work gives rise to ethical dilemmas rooted in dependency on others to facilitate movement in disaster-affected areas. Armaity Desai (2007) recounts how teachers and students from the TATA Institute had to negotiate with the police's wish to carry arms during their relief work in a minority area after the Mumbai Riots of 1992–3. They did not wish recipients to get the impression that their interventions were at odds with their stated aims of involving them as equal partners. The principle of non-involvement in the politics of any situation can be extremely trying at times. The Red Cross discovered that it was disempowered and could do little about the countless atrocities it witnessed during its attempts to provide succour to those caught in the civil war between the Fascists who supported Franco and Communists who were sustained by the International Brigade in the siege of Madrid during the Spanish Civil War (Sansom, 2006).

The case study below focuses on the Indian Ocean Tsunami because it illustrates how even devastating natural disasters could be mitigated by human action undertaken at an international level, e.g., providing preventative measures such as early warning systems.

Case study: The mobilization of social work organizations to assist people in disaster situations

On 26 December 2004, an earthquake off northwest Sumatra triggered a tsunami with waves 10 metres high that caused havoc in 12 countries bordering the Indian Ocean. Its impact was huge. In 2007, an American scientist calculated that the effects of the tsunami were felt as far away as the eastern seaboard of the USA and parts of the Canadian Maritimes. The tsunami killed 300,000 people and until 2008 stood as the natural disaster with the highest number of casualties in modern times. It brought forth unprecedented levels of goodwill and determination amongst ordinary people in scores of countries to help victim-survivors by sending funds and other resources (though social work educators like Gurid Askeland (2007) have asked whether reactions to this tsunami would be the same had it not included rich white Westerners on holiday amongst those afflicted). These gestures put governments to shame and they promptly followed suit with further promises of aid, often agreeing to match the large sums already donated by private citizens.

Social workers engaged with these initiatives as both private individuals and professionals. Amongst these were the International Association of Schools of Social Work (IASSW) and International Federation of Social Workers (IFSW). Their resources were limited, but they offered assistance to some of those affected. The IASSW formed the Rebuilding People's Lives Network (RIPL) for long-term reconstruction and the IFSW formed Families and Survivors of the Tsunami (FAST) to provide assistance and run workshops in Sri Lanka and Indonesia between December 2005 and August 2006 to train people and discuss intervention in relief efforts. Both projects were committed to engaging local people so that they determined how the disaster interventions would work out in practice. They offered themselves as 'brokers' who put people and resources together in ways that ensured local control of the relief processes and prioritized their wants – housing, schools and equipment to resume their livelihoods, usually fishing boats and outboard-motors.

The IASSW initiative in Sri Lanka soon realized the lack of capacity of social work to facilitate long-term community rebuilding processes. Lists of needs could be drawn up, but the expertise to coordinate community activities and build the networking relationships required to access resources not in the locale proved elusive. People living in affected villages are struggling to put their lives together many years after the event. The IASSW is committed to helping Sri Lanka develop its social work education infrastructure so that it can train the practitioners needed to do such work in future. This long-term initiative may take time to reach fruition, especially as resources have to be sought from other agencies, including governments. Its realization will become a practical manifestation of moving from saving lives to rebuilding livelihoods and shifting from disaster relief to long-term social development.

Intervening in such situations is difficult for social workers. Sri Lanka's rebuilding endeavours are complicated by civil unrest that long preceded the tsunami, but which impedes the smooth progress of aid through disputed parts of the territory as different actors seek to procure the allegiances of local people and take credit for developmental opportunities that are carried out. Social workers in such situations must make full use of their capacity to distance themselves from siding with any one party – their non-judgementalism and skills in conflict mediation and non-violent resolution of conflict create the space and freedom to contribute to rebuilding activities at local level.

Working with People in Disaster-Affected Areas

Social workers experienced in working in disaster-affected areas are keen to ensure that people affected by disasters are involved in decision-making and maintain control over their conditions as much as possible. The circumstances facing them are confused, full of ambiguities and lacking clear lines of responsibility. If mishandled, sensibilities could aggravate already tense and difficult situations. The social work values of equality, social justice, human rights, dignity and worth of individuals and communities are essential in working effectively with them. A belief in people's capacities to grow and develop if adequately supported also helps.

Drawing heavily on Desai (2007), I posit the skills and processes involved in working in disaster-affected communities below. They do not necessarily follow one another in a neat order, but often occur simultaneously and messily. They are:

- making initial contact;
- engaging local people throughout the processes of intervention;
- assessing available information and identifying areas of work;
- drawing up contracts for the work to be undertaken;
- initiating the required action(s); and
- constantly evaluating the results.

Making initial contact with people in the affected areas is a key first step. This is usually done in conjunction with others, including governments at national and local levels, depending on the social organization of a particular community, and other interested bodies, including non-governmental organizations (NGOs), that may already be in the area and have specific expertise and knowledge to contribute to rebuilding processes. Social workers coordinate activities with a wide range of organizations, individuals, families and communities. They collect information on the situation and assess needs and the resources available. Doing so requires them to engage sensitively with and talk directly to people affected so that their voices, often marginalized, are heard. The people concerned may be suffering stress from the trauma of the experience, loss of loved ones and lack of familiar material surroundings and belongings. They may be physically injured, in pain and requiring immediate medical attention.

As every moment counts, the data will have to be collected speedily, efficiently and accurately. People's lives may depend on the information conveyed through such an exercise. If they rely on others to assist in the data collection process, social workers have to know the politics of that particular area to figure out whether data are missing, e.g., people in conflict situations refusing to talk to those they consider 'enemies'. The politics of such situations require social workers to be cautious over how different community constituents see them and be aware that data accumulated may not be welcomed by all, especially if some groups feel responsible for what happened. Desai (2007) records how, following the gas explosion in Bhopal, India, that killed and injured thousands in 1984, data collected by social workers from the TATA Institute were suppressed by the government so as to protect the interests of the multinational corporation that owned the plant.

The information collected may need to be shared with many others – people affected by the disaster, governments, international organisations and NGOs. It provides the basis for: assessing losses or developing a census of loss; identifying the work that needs to be done, for whom it needs to be done and who should do it, according to skills held; and creating an inventory of materials needed. Policy, entitlements and courses of action to be followed may be decided on the basis of these data, so accuracy is crucial. It is important to identify and agree the roles to be taken by different actors and coordinate their diverse activities. Some players may want contracts to be signed before undertaking work, and these should be formalized prior to its commencement. Conflicts or differences of opinions over how work is to be conducted should be resolved to progress action for the benefit of local people.

Initiating contact with local people straightaway and involving them in all stages of a disaster intervention process is fundamental to good social work practice in affected areas. They are experts on the locality, including its cultures and traditions, who is who in a community, what its needs and resources are and how needs can best be met. Without their full participation, interventions may be harmful rather than beneficial. If people do not feel that they own what is being done, that is, they experience these actions as being done to them, they will not engage except in superficial ways for the sole purpose of accessing needed resources. Leaving people as bystanders in a process controlled by others might jeopardize long-term plans for reconstruction.

Social workers should be aware of tensions and social divisions in communities and prevent their distorting relief and rehabilitation efforts. People who are traditionally marginalized by existing structures may find that they continue to be disadvantaged under these initiatives unless specific steps are taken to counter their secondary status, engage them directly in what is going on and ensure that they receive their entitlements. Marginalization is often experienced by women in patriarchal groups, but this is seldom recognized in disaster relief operations. Engaging women requires a different approach that builds on women-only spaces and ring-fences resources for their use (Pittaway et al., 2007). Social workers should build on a community's existing efforts to include women. Knowing the specifics of gender relations in a locality will enable social workers to protect women's and children's interests in property if their husbands die in the disaster and safeguard their rights to assets that might be distributed, including those aimed at re-establishing livelihoods, e.g., fishing-boats and domestic animals. Otherwise, these goods might be appropriated by other family members who feel entitled to them or who might administer them on their behalf, thereby placing women and children in dependency relationships.

Other groups who may be excluded are senior citizens, orphaned children, disabled people and those who have no able-bodied men to care for them. Reconstruction efforts may require the creation of specific committees representing all community sectors to coordinate and advance work that has to be done. If these can be done at community, neighbourhood or village level, it is easier to ascertain whether everyone is involved. Agreeing housing designs to replace devastated homes can be a particularly protracted and contentious process and it is best to know the different requirements of various groups before discussions start. Social workers can facilitate the expression of particular preferences or advocate for solutions that marginalized people believe will meet their needs. In 2005, the American Federal Emergency Management Agency (FEMA) failed to engage poor African Americans in the aftermath of Hurricane Katrina in New Orleans and exposed the extra burdens that marginalized groups face in getting assistance during disasters, when they need help most.

That such marginalization could be perpetuated in a rich country shocked the world. In this case, FEMA replicated poor communities' marginalization rather than addressing it directly, and added to their hardship. Thus, few people who lived in poor neighbourhoods have returned to their devastated homes. Lower Ninth Ward, for example, has had 1,000 of its 14,000 residents return so far. In 2008, people continue to live in trailers provided by FEMA, surrounded by rubble and rubbish. Many are not eligible for the $150,000 in compensation offered under the Road Home Program because the state requires proof of ownership of homes that were destroyed, but much paper evidence was lost in the floods. Community activists have argued that this requirement is an unfair burden on former residents, but have yet to get it waived. Of 135,000 applications submitted, only 43,000 have been paid to date. Violence in the city has risen to an all-time high, much of it driven by the drug trade and failure of the police to re-establish its own infrastructure, including crime labs.

Initiating action and drawing upon various systems to conduct specific activities in the locality is an important part of recovery. The process can be protracted and last for years. In getting action going, the problems to be addressed have to be identified and possible solutions formulated. These might require people to be interviewed and asked for their opinions. Their views may be obtained in small group settings or at public meetings held especially for the purpose. People may be in a state of shock, anxious or otherwise traumatized, so care has to be taken when approaching them if they are not to be emotionally stressed further. Responses to the calamity are likely to be varied and can range from keeping busy – to the point of exhaustion and depression – to excessive consumption of alcohol or drugs. Fear, sadness and despair can be debilitating, making psychological support and mental health resources for survivors as important as material help. Helping people return to normal routines as quickly as possible is beneficial. If they work the land or are employed in factories, the delivery of relief supplies should be timed so as not to impede their carrying out these jobs.

Care has to be exercised to ensure that children are not neglected when responding to adult and community needs. Children can be assisted in transcending disaster events with various forms of therapy, including music therapy and play therapy. Under the guidance of adults sensitive to their needs, these can give them opportunities to express their feelings, reconstruct events and proceed with healing. Different strategies are essential for children of different ages and needs. Getting those of school age to re-engage with school work can assist them to move beyond the debilitating aspects of the disaster. They should be helped to get back to school as quickly as possible because their doing so can be advantageous in coming to terms with their experience. Obtaining support from peers can be useful if they have endured similar traumatic events. If children are missing, parents need help in finding them, while children who have been orphaned have to be found substitute families quickly, whether with kin or others. Otherwise, they become easy prey for exploitative adults who traffic and otherwise abuse them for sexual gratification, as occurred to children orphaned in the 2004 tsunami calamity. Though complicated by the strong belief that parents should be responsible for their children, appropriate limits have to be placed around adults' behaviour. It is important to consult children about decisions made on their behalf rather than facing them with those made by adults in an exercise of adult power or abuse of it. This becomes a form of oppression that I have termed *adultism* – the assumption that adults know what is best and can decide what will happen to children and young people without involving them.

Social workers engage in an iterative process of constantly evaluating and critically reflecting upon the effectiveness and results of their interventions. They consult with those involved in these actions to obtain their views about how well or badly these have gone alongside forming their own opinions of the success (or not) of their endeavours. They disseminate information about what they have been doing and the results of their evaluation to all stakeholders. They may need to participate in various forms of communication to reach different audiences when doing this, e.g., newspaper articles, flyers, posters, radio talks, TV shows, public meetings. If government policies are involved, they may get together with local dignitaries or elders and take a common message to the people. This may be important in explaining local people's rights to aid, listening to grievances about how it has been distributed in the immediate aftermath or planning initiatives for long-term reconstruction.

Social workers need specific training in disaster relief and reconstruction work to address the range of calamities that can strike anywhere, anytime. British courses pay little attention to this area and seldom cover it in today's overcrowded curriculum. General Social Care Council guidelines ignore this topic. Social services resources for working in this area are scarce. The flooding in England during the summer of 2007 revealed how ill prepared this industrial society is for dealing with the long-term effects of such catastrophes. Even here, people whose homes were badly damaged may take years to recover. Helping people in these circumstances obtain resources – material and emotional – to rebuild their lives is something that social workers have the skills to do.

It is not just the victims of disaster themselves who are traumatized, however. Working in disaster-affected areas can leave lasting impressions on social workers, too. Some of what they see and information gathered may be extremely distressing. Social workers have to be prepared to deal with these in an appropriate manner to avoid debilitating themselves or becoming burnt out by the sadness and tragedies they encounter. The parallels with child protection work are evident. As in that, supervision is essential in providing support when doing disaster relief work. If they find the situation too much to bear, social workers will need the courage to leave and let others do this work. This is not a dishonourable position to adopt. Everyone has his or her personal limits.

Conclusions

Social workers have enormous challenges to face in responding to people's needs during disaster relief situations. Working in this area draws upon all their values, skills and technical knowledge – political, social, cultural and economic. They work across many divides that separate people from one another and hinder cooperative endeavours that could serve all their interests. Social workers are skilled at navigating their way through conflicts while retaining the dignity of those they are negotiating with and maintaining their own integrity. They need training and research to keep tabs on new research and knowledge. Working in areas devastated by disasters requires strength, courage and fortitude. Relief workers' lives may be endangered by their willingness to serve others. This has happened to Red Cross workers in many situations, including Iraq and countries in Africa. Even those working in official capacities for the United Nations may also lose their lives, as many did in Iraq.

Social workers can support people affected by disasters, in the short term to bring succour to individuals, and in the long term to reconstruct communities. They can assist in creating and implementing forward-looking preventive and preparedness measures that can mitigate the effects of potential disasters. Such endeavours can be considered long-term interventions that begin in the here and now. Forward planning for events that may never happen involves taking action that can mitigate current and potential risks and offers one way of approaching this task. Social action that builds inclusive networks of solidarity and encourages social cohesion can help to embed existing social capital in wider social relationships. The constant evolution and extension of social capital through the formation of social networks that engage people in social interactions with each other can also secure their futures. If rooted in calls for social justice and human rights, such responses can enhance individual and community capacities and skills. Social workers also need to look after themselves. Self-care is essential in avoiding stress and burnout in trying circumstances.

Conclusions

Universal Services for All or Residual Services for the Few?

Social work has an important, if at times ambiguous and challenging, role in responding to its core business – enhancing people's well-being across the life-course. Social workers are charged with carrying out this vital task by working with a range of other professionals and volunteers. Realizing social work's remit calls for highly skilled practitioners to assess situations, manage ambiguity and complexity in service users' lives and implement change at personal and/or structural levels (Mullaly, 2002). As professionals, they deal with some of the most damaged people in society and seek solutions to intractable social problems: child abuse, elder abuse, mental ill health, homelessness, substance misuse, disasters. To tackle these they require specific knowledge in several disciplines, wide-ranging skills and a capacity to intervene sensitively in tough situations. Social workers operate singly or work in partnerships with others. Constant changes in public policies have direct consequences for practice, including integration between different helping professionals and working to common assessment frameworks as key aspects of the modernization of public services. As social workers participate in a contested profession, their activities are in continuous flux and easily appropriated by other practitioners. Disputes about who pays for care, e.g., over bed-blocking, only complicate the situation.

Social workers' extensive skills in addressing complex problems are under-rated because of the linked and blurred boundaries between formal or professional social work and informal care. In the UK, political deci-sion-makers have aggressively undermined social work endeavours, devalued training requirements and ignored the profession's low status for years. Virgina Bottomley, when Secretary of State responsible for the profession, verbalized popular visions of social workers' capacities as rooted in the mundane and unskilled activities of daily living. The senti-ments would be laughable were they not articulated by a powerful opinion-former. The belief that anyone can do social work formalizes the perception that social workers need no professional training, or only a low level of it. New Labour's replacement of the two-year diploma with a three-year degree could be interpreted as political enthusiasm for social work. While an improvement, however, it lacks coherence or structures that link training at all levels to career progression. Gover-nance mechanisms are also inadequate. Arrangements in the USA provide a counter-example to learn from. There, the Council for Social Work Education (CSWE), a membership organization with decades of experi-ence in accrediting social work programmes, has a ladder of training. Basic qualifying training occurs at Bachelor's level; specialist training at Master's. A Ph.D. prepares those who will teach in universities or manage social work agencies. Nevertheless, despite its strengths, the American welfare system is problematic in that its market-dominated social services exclude poor people.

Social workers have powers to deny people's liberty and enforce com-pliance with court orders. Their interventions are not always appreciated by those receiving services, employers or the public. Service users are stigmatized and facilities accessed are depicted as residual and relevant only for those unable to provide for themselves. Like service users, social workers can be stigmatized too. Jonathan Parker (2007a, 2007b) calls this 'stigmatization through association'. Some people wishing to access the personal social services are unable to do so because they belong to an 'undeserving' group or are not considered vulnerable or entitled to them. Some adult men and women in need of assistance can be in this category, e.g., women surviving domestic abuse by men partners. Without statutory obligations for this group, meeting their needs is left to under-resourced voluntary agencies.

In this chapter, I argue that it is time to rethink the personal social services and debate their provision as universal goods available to all in need. In an interdependent world subject to human or natural calamities and heavily polluted by industrial processes, action has to be undertaken at local, national and international levels to sustain human well-being. Involving social workers in the processes of planning to avert problems in both individual and societal spheres can enhance the quality of life for all on earth.

Contemporary Challenges for Social Workers to Address

Contemporary challenges for social workers include globalization, migration, organized crime, the drug trade, human trafficking, armed conflicts, natural and man-made disasters and widespread poverty. These shape individual and collective lives and social workers' responses to those requiring assistance. How these forces influenced practice can be exemplified by focusing on poverty.

Poverty, a key concern in social work as 80 per cent of service users are on low incomes, is rising globally. The gap between rich and poor is growing everywhere: in rich industrialized countries like the UK; emergent economies in India, China, Brazil and Eastern Europe; and industrializing ones located mainly in the southern hemisphere. The number of individuals owning much of the world's wealth is small, leaving the bulk of the world's population to make do with a meagre portion of it. According to *Forbes* magazine, 946 individuals are multi-billionaires who accumulated a total of $US3.5 trillion in 2007 (Kroll and Fass, 2007). Most are men; 40 per cent are American. Despite global commitments to eradicating poverty – e.g., the UN's Millennium Development Goals, which have social workers involved in their implementation – income inequalities remain a huge issue. Poverty exacerbates social exclusion and conflicts over the distribution of the world's resources and growing inequalities make social work interventions more difficult. In the UK, for example, New Labour has expended considerable sums on eradicating child poverty to enhance children's well-being and realize *Every Child Matters*. Its failure to meet this objective makes supporting poor children and families immensely more complicated as individual needs and structural failings deepen and intensify the crises they face.

Social workers are expected to deal with the consequences of such inequalities, so I turn to examine how the three key approaches to social work – maintenance, therapeutic and emancipatory – would respond to the problem and position social workers in debates about what to do. The maintenance approach would deem dealing with issues of poverty an individual matter and focus on assisting a person to improve his or her uptake of benefits, employment skills and training needs without being concerned about the structural dimensions of poverty like the unequal distribution of wealth, low pay or lack of jobs with pay levels that would enable people to rise out of poverty. Adherents of this approach might acknowledge the presence of such problems, but would expect other professionals and politicians to address these, mainly because they define these as political rather than professional concerns. By drawing narrow boundaries around their role, they would not perceive their ignoring these matters as a political act.

The therapeutic approach would focus on interpersonal relationships within the family and amongst peer groups, particularly the failure of parents to offer good role models to children, enforce discipline and encourage working hard at school in preparation for employment and a better life later. Adherents of this approach might identify a 'cycle of deprivation' whereby several generations of one family seem incapable of moving out of poverty and encourage its members to improve their relationships with one another, widen their social networks and access educational opportunities and jobs that would enable them to enter a more life-enhancing environment. Like maintenance workers, they would not focus on structural inequalities as a concern for them to tackle.

The emancipatory approach, especially its holistic variant, seeks to address individual and structural problems because it views dealing with both as integral to enhancing individual and community well-being. The practice of this approach at the individual level does not differ substantially from that of the other two approaches. The emancipatory practitioner would also see deprivation as a problem of being workless and encourage people to improve their relationships with one another and get education and training to increase their potential to compete in the labour market. However, they would also define caring as socially useful work and would want this recognized. For example, in helping to improve the life chances of women looking after children, they would work with others to argue for policy changes such as raising benefit levels for these carers rather than taking them as given. And they would lobby for a more equitable sharing of the world's wealth and physical and social resources. Promoting social work as both a political and a moral profession would embroil them in various controversies, including arguing for universal services, challenging taxation policies, addressing global interdependencies that have precipitated current crises for poor people like rising food and fuel prices, and working to prevent diseases that have a global reach. Thus, they would work at the individual, national and international levels.

Stigmatized, Residual Services for the Few or High-Quality Universal Services for Everyone?

The prospects of arguing for universal services today are bleak, and emancipatory social workers face an uphill task. They could engage in organizational and policy changes by beginning to debate alternative arrangements. Collaborating with economists, they could show how higher taxes on a graduated scale could pay for universal social services embedded in high-quality publicly funded care. They would research the impact of poverty and social exclusion to acquire evidence for moving in this direction. Crucial to their arguments will be demonstrating the exclusionary effects of user fees on those with low incomes.

Existing arrangements for the personal social services in Britain are part of a welfare state funded through taxation. Pooling risks and resources to enable a person needing support to be financed by all workers drew on social solidarity and reciprocity as the basis for non-stigmatized services within a social insurance system and public funding. These have never been funded adequately, even at their formation. The Treasury rejected William Beveridge's suggestion of the personal social services as the fifth universal service (Kincaid, 1973). Low levels of funding have targeted facilities to those most in need, and turned them into stigmatized, residual services that people request as a last resort. The frustrations of those for whom social workers have no resources are counterbalanced by those praising their efforts in providing practical social work help in difficult circumstances (Beresford et al., 2006).

Politicians in the UK and the West in general have bought the idea that the public is not willing to pay taxes to fund social services. However, several surveys show that the British public and people in other nations favour the idea of a welfare state supported through taxation to fund specific services like health and education. Yet their universality is being undermined through user fees. Prescription charges, dental fees, fees for eye tests and charges for community care exemplify this. User fees exclude people on low income from services that are too expensive for them, even if subsidized. For example, older people in England pay for residential care because it is classified a social services responsibility, not a health one. Under the capital disregard rules clarified in 1999, a person with more than £16,000 (raised to £21,500 in 2007) in capital assets has to sell these to pay for their care. This policy is problematic for service users and carers on low incomes. The funds raised may not cover the whole of their care if they live a long life and costs continue to rise.

The sale of their home can cause much hardship and despair if shared with carers who are not a spouse. It can impact upon intergenerational relations because low-income older people cannot bequeath a house to children who lack the means to buy their own. The capital disregard affects poor older people more than wealthy ones because their home constitutes proportionately more of their assets and they lack other wealth to cushion the blow as do wealthy people. These older people may be covered by means-tested provisions, but they tend to dislike these as they are usually stigmatized.

Creating the personal social services as publicly funded universal provisions ensures that no one has to make do, worry about being unable to pay or receive stigmatized services. Achieving this objective means establishing a political commitment to solidarity, social justice and pooling social resources for the good of all. In the current climate emancipatory social workers would have to convince politicians to accept a new relationship between individuals and the state and argue that a duty to care and right to receive care applies to both sides in a caring equation. It would also mean redefining accessing social resources to enable individuals to develop their full potential as a social responsibility, not the individual one popularized by Thatcherite ideology. Finally, it would mean valuing caring not linked to the labour market. This is extensive. Age Concern has estimated that older people contribute more than £24 billion in unpaid work to the British economy. This includes: £15.2 billion by carers over 50; £3.9 billion by grandparents doing childcare; and £5 billion from voluntary work.

Creating the personal social services as a universal right will be an uphill, but not impossible, struggle under neo-liberalism and a culture of individual self-sufficiency. Making these services universal requires more revenue to pay for them, highlighting a problematic relationship between taxation and welfare goods. Changing current funding arrangements requires wide-ranging taxation and policy reforms to make the burden of taxation fairer. Policy changes would have to cover income tax, inheritance tax and corporation tax. Corporation taxes in the UK are low, with only 10 per cent for venture equity capital. Tax avoidance schemes by the super-rich cost the Treasury £13 billion yearly. If collected, this could increase old age pensions by 20 per cent (Mathiason, 2008: 1) and alleviate pensioner poverty. A welfare state funded through taxation could still leave a mix of service providers in the public, private and voluntary sectors.

In arguing for an alternative vision, social workers can use research to show how people's daily lives are stunted by social exclusion, failure to 'make it in the market' and a devalued assessment of skills used in everyday life practices. Social workers can research and expose the social costs of having disenfranchised, alienated groups, especially young people who see no future for themselves and become disenchanted with following social norms from which they do not benefit. Hopelessness in such situations increases the lure of criminal pursuits, including drug abuse, violent gun crime and organized gangs. Doing nothing about such situations would condemn additional generations of children to not fulfilling their potential, despite the UK's commitment to international protocols like the Convention on the Rights of the Child, which requires the state to provide the resources necessary for children to grow.

Emancipatory approaches encourage critical reflective practitioners to use social work values, knowledge and skills to solve intractable problems and include those at society's margins. Social workers can assist marginalized groups and communities to articulate their dreams, get their voices heard in political circles, begin a journey for change that supports their well-being and question social priorities. These would aim to ensure that a stakeholder society gives *all stakeholders an equal place and voice* at decision-making tables and promotes an *equitable share of social resources*.

Emancipatory social workers challenge all of us to think differently about how we enhance the well-being of current residents of this planet and future generations in a world that is increasingly interdependent. The diversity of the world – its flora, fauna and peoples – will not survive without cooperation for the benefit of all. Universal services that are inclusive, without stigma, can enable society to care for all residents. Social workers can use their values and skills to transform social relations in egalitarian directions.

Bibliography

Askeland, G. (2007) 'Globalisation and a Flood of Travellers: Flooded Travellers and Social Justice', in L. Dominelli (ed.), *Revitalising Communities in a Globalising World*. Aldershot: Ashgate.

Bailey, R. and Brake, M. (eds) (1975) *Radical Social Work*. London: Edward Arnold.

Banks, S. (2002) 'Professional Values and Accountabilities', in R. Adams, L. Dominelli and M. Payne (eds), *Critical Practice in Social Work*. Basingstoke: Palgrave.

Banks, S. (2006) *Values and Ethics in Social Work*. 3rd edition. London: Palgrave.

Barclay, P. (1982) *The Barclay Report: Social Workers, Their Roles and Tasks*. London: NISW/MacDonald and Evans.

Batty, D. (2001) 'Council Slated for Substandard Adoption Proceedings', *The Guardian, Society*, 24 October.

Batty, D. (2004) 'People with Mental Illness Face Widespread Discrimination', *The Guardian*, 28 April.

Bauman, Z. (2000) 'Issues of Law and Order', *British Journal of Criminology*, 40: 205–21.

BBC News (2001) Road Protest Over Care Homes. 2 June. *http://news.bbc.co.uk/1/hi/health/1363762.stm*. Accessed 24 July 2008.

BBC News (2003a) Doctors Suspended over Patients' Deaths. 2 July. *http://news.bbc.co.uk/1/hi/england/west_midlands/3038612.stm*. Accessed 14 August 2008.

BBC News (2003b) Disabled Student Wins College Fight. 2 September. *http://news.bbc.co.uk/1/hi/england/london/3201927.stm*. Accessed 15 August 2008.

BBC News (2006) Churchill Sculpture Sparks Uproar. 11 March. *http://news.bbc.co.uk/1/hi/uk/4795832.stm*. Accessed 18 August 2008.

Beck, U. (1992) *Risk Society: Towards a New Modernity*. London: Sage.

Beck, U. (1999) *World Risk Society*. Cambridge: Polity Press.

Begum, N. (1992) 'Disabled Women and the Feminist Agenda', *Feminist Review*, 40: 71–84.

Bell, S. (1985) *When Salem Came to the 'Boro*. London: Pan Books.

Berardi, B., Leggieri, G., Manchetti, M. and Ferrari, G. (1999) 'Collaboration between Mental Health Services and Primary Care: The Bologna Project', *Journal of Clinical Psychiatry*, 1(6): 180–3.

Beresford, P., Adshead, L. and Croft, S. (2006) *Palliative Care, Social Work and Service Users: Making Life Possible*. London: Jessica Kingsley Publishers.

Bhopal, R. (1998) 'Spectre of Racism in Health and Health Care: Lessons from History and the United States', *British Medical Journal*, 316: 1970–3.

Biestek, F.P. (1961) *The Casework Relationship*. London: Allen and Unwin.

Brown, G. and Harris, T. (1978) *The Social Origins of Depression*. London: Tavistock.

Butler-Sloss, E. (1988) *The Report of the Inquiry into Child Abuse in Cleveland, 1987*. Cmnd 412. London: HMSO.

Callahan, M., Dominelli, L., Rutman, D. and Strega, S. (2003) 'Undeserving Mothers: Lived Experiences of Young Mothers in and from Government Care', in K. Kulfeldt and B. McKenzie (eds), *Child Welfare: Connecting Research, Policy and Practice*. Waterloo, Ont.: Wilfrid Laurier University Press.

Campbell, B. (1997) *Unofficial Secrets: Child Sexual Abuse and the Cleveland Case. Ten Years After*. London: Virago.

Carter, P. (2003) *Managing Offenders, Reducing Crime: A New Approach*. London: Home Office.

Challis, D. and Davies, B. (1986) *Case Management in Community Care*. Aldershot: Gower.

Cherry, P. (2007) '14-Year-Old Montreal Girl Beaten to Death, Police Say', *National Post*, 21 August.

Cigno, K. (2002) 'Cognitive-Behaviour Practice', in R. Adams, L. Dominelli and M. Payne (eds), *Social Work: Themes, Issues and Critical Debates*. 2nd edition. London: Palgrave/Macmillan. (First published 1998.)

Clode, C. (2001) Consultation on Social Services Draft Code: A One-Sided Code? Freedom to Care. *http://www.dh.gov.uk/en/Consultations/Liveconsultations/DH_079842*. Accessed 14 August 2008.

Cohen, S. (2001) *Immigration Controls, the Family and the State: A Handbook of Law, Theory, Politics and Practice for Local Authority, Voluntary Sector Welfare State Workers and Legal Advisors*. London: Jessica Kingsley Publishers.

Commission for Social Care Inspection (CSCI) (2003) *Report into Private Nursing Homes*. London: CSCI.

Compton, B. and Galaway, B. (2006) *Social Work Processes*. 6th edition. Homewood, Ill.: The Dorsey Press.

Criminal Justice Board (CJB) (2007) *Black Minority Ethnic Staffing Data*. London: CJB.

Davies, M. (1985) *The Essential Social Worker*. Aldershot: Gower.

Department for Education and Skills (DfES) (2004) *Every Child Matters: Change for Children in Social Care*. London: DfES.

Department for Education and Skills (DfES) (2006) *Working Together to Safeguard Children: A Guide to Inter-Agency Working to Safeguard and Promote the Welfare of Children*. London: The Stationery Office.

Department of Environment, Transport and the Regions (DETR) (1998) *Modern Local Government: In Touch with People*. Cmnd 4014. London: The Stationery Office.

Department of Health (DH) (1998) *Modernising Social Services*. Cmnd 4169. London: The Stationery Office.

Department of Health (DH) (1999) *Modernising Mental Health Services: Safe, Sound and Supportive*. London: DH.

Department of Health (DH) (2000) *Framework for the Assessment of Children in Need and Their Families*. London: The Stationery Office.

Department of Health (DH) (2001a) *The National Service Framework for Older People*. London: HMSO.

Department of Health (DH) (2001b) *Valuing People*. London: DH.

Department of Health (DH) (2002a) *Fair Access to Care Services: Policy Guidance*. London: DH.

Department of Health (DH) (2002b) *Requirements for Social Work Training*. London: DH.

Department of Health (DH) (2002c) *The Single Assessment Process: Guidance for Local Implementation*. London: DH.

Department of Health (DH) (2003) *Every Child Matters: The Green Paper*. London: DH.

Department of Health (DH) (2005) *Independence, Well-Being and Choice: Our Vision for the Future of Social Care for Adults in England*. Cmnd 6499. London: DH.

Department of Health (DH) (2006) *Our Health, Our Care, Our Say: A New Direction for Community Services*. London: DH.

Department of Health (DH) (2007) *Drug Misuse and Dependency: Guidance in Clinical Management*. London: DH.

Desai, A. (2007) 'Disaster and Social Work Responses', in L. Dominelli (ed.), *Revitalising Communities in a Globalising World*. Aldershot: Ashgate.

Devo, J. (2006) 'Out of Africa into Birmingham: Zimbabwean Social Workers Talk to *Professional Social Work*', *Professional Social Work*, 1 August, pp. 12–13.

Disability Rights Commission (DRC) (2004) Manchester City Council v. (1) Romano & (2) Samari 2004 EWCA Civ 834. DRC – Intervener. *http://83.137.212.42/sitearchive/drc/the_law/drc_legal_cases/interventions/manchester_city_council_-v-_1.html*. Accessed 15 August 2008.

Dodd, V. and Wintour, P. (2005) 'Tories Plan HIV Tests for Migrants', *The Guardian*, 15 February.

Dodd, V. and Wintour, P. (2006) 'BNP Needs 5% Swing to Win 70 Council Seats', *The Guardian*, 17 April.

Dominelli, L. (1988) *Anti-Racist Social Work*. London: BASW/Macmillan; 2nd edition, 1997; 3rd edition, 2008.

Dominelli, L. (1997) *Sociology for Social Work*. London: Macmillan.

Dominelli, L. (2002a) *Anti-Oppressive Social Work Theory and Practice*. London: Palgrave/Macmillan.

Dominelli, L. (2002b) *Feminist Social Work Theory and Practice*. London: Palgrave/Macmillan.

Dominelli, L. (2002c) 'Values in Social Work: Contested Entities with Enduring Qualities', in R. Adams, L. Dominelli and M. Payne (eds), *Critical Practice in Social Work*. London: Palgrave.

Dominelli, L. (2004a) *Social Work: Theory and Practice for a Changing Profession*. Cambridge: Polity Press.

Dominelli, L. (2004b) 'Practising Social Work in a Globalizing World', in N.T. Tan and A. Rowlands (eds), *Social Work Around the World III*. Berne: IFSW.

Dominelli, L. (2006) *Women and Community Action*. Bristol: Policy Press.

Dominelli, L. and Hoogvelt, A. (1996) 'Globalisation and the Technocratisation of Social Work', *Critical Social Policy*, 16(2): 45–62.

Dominelli, L., Strega, S., Callahan, M. and Rutman, D. (2005) 'Endangered Children: The State as Parent and Grandparent', *British Journal of Social Work*, 35(7): 1123–44.

Double, D. (2005) *Critical Psychiatry: Limits of Madness*. New York and London: Palgrave/Macmillan.

Dunant, S. (ed.) (1994) *The War of the Words: The Political Correctness Debate*. London: Virago.

Fawcett Society (2007) *Evidence from the Fawcett Society to the Home Affairs Committee Inquiry on Sentencing*. London: Fawcett Society.

Fernando, S. (1991) *Health, 'Race' and Culture*. London: Macmillan.

Fernando, S. (2001) *Cultural Diversity: Mental Health and Psychiatry. The Struggle against Racism*. London: Routledge.

Fleming, P., Bamford, D. and McCaughley, N. (2005) 'An Exploration of the Health and Social Wellbeing Needs of Looked After Young People: A Multi-Method Approach', *Journal of Interprofessional Care*, 19(1): 35–49.

Folgheraiter, F. (2004) *Relational Social Work: Toward Network and Societal Practices*. London: Jessica Kingsley Publishers.

Fooks, J. (2002) *Social Work: Critical Theory and Practice*. London: Sage.

Foucault, M. (1991) 'Governmentality', in G. Burchell, C. Gordon and P. Miller (eds), *The Foucault Effect: Studies in Governmentality*. Hemel Hempstead: Harvester/Wheatsheaf.

Furniss, E. (1995) *Victims of Benevolence: The Dark Legacy of the Williams Lake Residential School*. Vancouver: Arsenal Pulp Press.

General Social Care Council (GSCC) (2008) *Raising Standards: Social Work Conduct in England 2003–2008*. London: GSCC.

Goffman, E. (1961) *Asylums: Essays on the Social Situation of Mental Patients and Other Inmates*. Harmondsworth: Penguin.

Golightley, M. (2006) *Social Work and Mental Health*. Exeter: Learning Matters Ltd.

Goodchild, S. (2002) 'Public to Foot Bill for £100 million Yarl's Wood Fire', *The Independent*, 7 April.

Gordon, L. (2006) *The Economic and Social Costs of Class A Drug Use in England and Wales*. London: Home Office.

Graef, R. (1992) *Living Dangerously: Young Offenders in Their Own Words*. London: HarperCollins.

Graham, M. (2006) *Black Perspectives in Social Work*. Bristol: Policy Press.

Greer, P. (1994) *Transforming Central Government: The Next Steps Initiatives*. London: Open University Press.

Griffiths, R. (1988) *Community Care, the Agenda for Action* (also known as *The Griffiths Report*). London: HMSO.

Haines, K. (2002) 'Youth Offenders and Youth Justice', in R. Adams, L. Dominelli and M. Payne (eds), *Critical Practice in Social Work*. London: Macmillan/Palgrave.

Healthcare Commission and Commission for Social Care Inspection (HC and CSCI) (2006) *Joint Investigation into Services for Learning Disabled People in a Cornwall Partnership Trust*. London: HC.

Her Majesty's Prison Service (HMPS) (2007) Contracted Out Prisons. *http://www.hmprisonservice.gov.uk/prisoninformation/privateprison/*. Accessed 24 July 2008.

Higham, P. (2005) What is Important About Social Work and Social Care? Paper for The Assembly in Social Work and Social Care Meeting, 14 March.

Horner, N. (2007) *What is Social Work? Context and Perspectives*. Exeter: Learning Matters.

Hough, M., Clancy, A., McSweeney, T. and Turnbull, P.J. (2003) 'The Impact of Drug Treatment and Testing Orders on Offending: Two Year Reconviction Results', *Home Office Findings No. 184*. London: Home Office.

International Association of Schools of Social Work and International Federation of Social Workers (IASSW–IFSW) (2004) *The Global Standards and Ethical Document*. Southampton: IASSW–IFSW. Considered at the IASSW–IFSW Joint Congress in Adelaide, Australia, 4–8 October.

Jaggi, M., Muller, R. and Schmid, S. (1977) *Red Bologna*. London: Writers and Readers Cooperative.

Javadian, R. (2007) 'Social Work Responses to Earthquake Disasters: A Social Work Intervention in Bam, Iran', *International Social Work*, 50(3): 334–46.

John-Baptiste, A. (2001) 'Appropriateness of Social Work Practice with Communities of African Origin', in L. Dominelli, W. Lorenz and H. Soydan (eds), *Beyond Racial Divides: Ethnicities in Social Work*. Aldershot: Ashgate.

Kassindja, F. and Miller-Basher, L. (1998) *Do They Hear You When You Cry?* New York: Delacourt Press.

Kendall, K. (1978) *Reflections on Social Work Education, 1950–1978*. New York: IASSW.

Kendall, K. (2000) *Social Work Education: Its Origins in Europe*. Alexandra, Va.: CSWE.

Kennedy, M. (2000) 'Christianity and Child Sexual Abuse: The Survivors' Voice Leading to Change', *Child Abuse Review*, 9(2): 124–41.

Kincaid, J. (1973) *Poverty and Inequality in Britain*. Harmondsworth: Penguin.

Kirkwood, A. (1993) *The Leicestershire Inquiry 1992*. Leicester: Leicestershire County Council.

Knott, C. (2006) *National Offender Management Service (NOMS): Working Together to Reduce Re-Offending: The NOMS Management Model*. London: NOMS.

Kornstein, S.G. and Clayton, A. (eds) (2002) *Women's Mental Health*. New York: The Guilford Press.

Kroll, L. and Fass, L. (2007) 'The World's Richest People', *Forbes Magazine*, 8 March. *http://www.forbes.com/2007/03/06/billionaires-new-richest_07billionaires_cz_lk_af_0308billieintro.html*. Accessed 24 July 2008.

Laing, R.D. (1969) *Intervention in Social Situations*. London: Association of Family Caseworkers/Philadelphia Association Ltd.

Laing, W. (2004) *Calculating a Fair Price for Care: A Toolkit for Residential and Nursing Care Costs*. 2nd edition. Bristol: Policy Press/JRF.

Laming, H. (2003) *The Inquiry into Victoria Climbié*. London: The Stationery Office.

Levy, A. and Kahan, B. (1991) *The Pindown Experience and the Protection of Children: The Report of the Staffordshire Child Care Inquiry, 1990*. Stafford: Staffordshire County Council.

Lewis, J. and Glennerster, H. (1996) *Implementing the New Community Care*. Buckingham: Open University Press.

Like Minds (2007) Like Minds/Like Mine. *http://www.likeminds.org.nz*. Accessed 24 July 2008.

Littlewood, R. and Lipsedge, M. (1997) *The Aliens and the Alienists*. London: Routledge.

Lymbery, M. (2005) *Social Work with Older People: Context, Policy and Practice*. London: Sage.

Lyon, J., Dennison, C. and Wilson, A. (2000) *'Tell Them so They Listen': Messages from Young People in Custody*. London: Home Office, Study 201.

McLeod, S. (1982) *The Art of Starvation*. New York: Schocken.

Macpherson, W. (1999) *Report of the Stephen Lawrence Inquiry: Report of an Inquiry by Sir William Macpherson of Cluny*. Cmnd 4262. London: The Stationery Office.

Malin, N. (ed.) (1995) *Services for People with Learning Disabilities*. London: Routledge.

Maquire, M. and Dewing, H. (2007) 'New Psychoanalytic Theories of Female and Male Femininity: The Oedipus Complex, Language and Gender Embodiment', *British Journal of Psychotherapy*, 23(4): 531–45.

Marshall, T.H. (1970) *Social Policy in the Twentieth Century*. London: Hutchinson.

Mathiason, N. (2008) 'Tax Avoidance by UK's Super-Rich "Worth £13bn"', *The Observer, Business and Media*, 27 January.

Moriarty, J. and Levin, E. (1998) 'Respite Care in Homes and Hospitals', in R. Jack (ed.), *Residential Versus Community Care*. London: Macmillan.

Morris, J. (2006) *Centres for Independent Living; Local User-Led Organisations*. London: Valuing People Support Team.

Mullaly, R. (2002) *Structural Social Work*. Toronto: McClelland and Stuart.

Munoz, M. (2007) 'Peru Earthquake', *The Vancouver Sun*, 16 August.

National Council for Voluntary Organizations (NCVO) and UK Workforce Hub (WH) (2007) *UK Voluntary Sector Workforce Almanac*. London: NCVO.

National Offender Management Service (NOMS) (2006) *Improving Prison and Probation Services: Public Value Partnerships*. London: Home Office/NOMS.

Nazroo, J. (1999) *Ethnicity and Mental Health*. London: Policy Studies Institute.

Office of National Statistics (ONS) (2001) *Children Accommodated in Secure Units by 31 March 2000 in England and Wales*. London: ONS Statistical Bulletin.

Office of National Statistics (ONS) (2005) *Adult Social Services Statistics*. London: ONS.

Oliver, M. (1990) *The Politics of Disability*. London: Macmillan.

Open Mind (1980) 'Community Mental Health Services in China', *Open Mind*, October.

Orme, J. (2001) *Gender and Community Care: Social Work and Social Care Perspectives*. London: Palgrave.

Parker, H., Aldridge, J. and Measham, F. (1998) *Illegal Leisure: The Normalisation of Adolescent Recreational Drug Use*. London: Routledge.

Parker, J. (2007a) 'Disadvantage, Stigma and Anti-Oppressive Practice', in P. Burke and J. Parker (eds), *Social Work and Disadvantage: Addressing the Roots of Stigma by Association*. London: Jessica Kingsley Publishers.

Parker, J. (2007b) *Disability and Stigma by Association*. London: Macmillan/Palgrave.

Parton, N. (1998) 'Risk, Advanced Liberalism and Child Welfare: The Need to Rediscover Uncertainty and Ambiguity', *British Journal of Social Work*, 28(1): 5–27.

Payne, M. (2005) *Modern Social Work Theory*. 3rd edition. London: Palgrave.

Phillipson, C. (1982) *Capitalism and the Construction of Old Age*. London: Macmillan.

Pilger, J. (2005) 'The Other Tsunami', *New Statesman*, 10 January. *http://www.newstatesman.com/200501100003*. Accessed 15 August 2008.

Pittaway, E., Bartolomei, L. and Rees, S. (2007) 'Gendered Dimensions of the 2004 Tsunami and a Potential Social Work Response in Post-Disaster Situations', *International Social Work*, 50(3): 307–19.

Pringle, K. (1995) *Men, Masculinities and Social Welfare*. London: UCL Press.

Prochaska, J.O., Diclemente, C.C. and Norcross, J.C. (1992) 'In Search of How People Change: Applications to Addictive Behaviours', *American Psychologist*, 47(9): 1102–14.

Prochaska, J.O., Diclemente, C.C. and Norcross, J.C. (1994) *Changing for Good*. New York: Avon Books.

Quinsey, V.L. (1995) 'Predicting Sexual Offences: Assessing Dangerousness', in J.C. Campbell (ed.), *Violence by Sex Offenders, Batterers and Child Abusers*. London: Sage.

Ray, M. and Phillips, J. (2002) 'Older People', in R. Adams, L. Dominelli and M. Payne (eds), *Critical Practice in Social Work*. London: Palgrave.

Raymond, V. (2007) 'Rat Boy Tearaway Finds God', *Sunday Mirror*, 3 June.

Refugee Council (2006) *The Impact Report*. London: Refugee Council.

Refugee Council (2007) *Refugees' Experiences of Education*. London: Refugee Council.

Riga, A. (2007) 'Mennonites Threaten to Abandon Quebec', *The Vancouver Sun*, 16 August.

Rook, K. (2007) 'Adoptive Mother Wants to Take Case for Maternity Benefits to Top Court', *The Vancouver Sun*, 16 August.

Rosenberg, M. (2007) '46 Kids Found in Illegal Foster Home', *The Vancouver Sun*, 13 August.

Russo, H. (1988) *Disabled, Female and Proud: Ten Stories of Women with Disabilities*. Boston: Exceptional Parent Press.

Rutman, D., Strega, S., Callahan, M. and Dominelli, L. (2002) 'Undeserving Mothers? Practitioners' Experiences Working with Young Mothers In/ From Care', *Child and Family Social Work*, 7(1): 149–59.

Sansom, C.J. (2006) *Winter in Madrid*. London: Macmillan.

Seebohm, F. (1968) *The Seebohm Report. Reports of the Committee on Local Authority and Allied Personal Social Services*. Cmnd 3703. London: HMSO.

Sefton, T. (2007) *Report on Unclaimed Benefits for Older People*. London: Help the Aged.

Segal, E., Gerdes, K. and Steiner, S. (2004) *Social Work: An Introduction to the Profession*. Belmont, Calif.: Thomson Books.

Shakespeare, T. (1999) 'When Is a Man Not a Man? When He's Disabled', in J. Wild (ed.), *Working with Men for Change*. London: UCL Press.

Sinoski, K. (2007) 'Taxi Firm Settles with Blind Man Refused Ride Because of Guide Dog', *The Vancouver Sun*, 16 August.

Small, J. (1987) 'Transracial Placements: Conflicts and Contradictions', in S. Ahmed, J. Cheetham and J. Small (eds), *Social Work with Black Children and Their Families*. London: Batsford.

Stanley, N. (2005) 'The Mental Health of Looked After Children: Matching Response to Need', *Health and Social Care in the Community*, 13(3): 239–48.

Strega, S. (2004) The Case of the Missing Perpetrator. Ph.D. thesis. Southampton University, Social Work Studies.

Strega, S., Callahan, M., Rutman, D. and Dominelli, L. (2002) 'Undeserving Mothers: Social Policy and Disadvantaged Mothers', *Canadian Review of Social Policy/Revue Canadienne de Politique Sociale*, 40–50: 175–94.

Sunderland, S. (1999) *With Respect to Old Age: Long-Term Care – Rights and Responsibilities: A Report of the Royal Commission on Long-Term Care*. London: The Stationery Office.

Szasz, T. (1972) *The Myth of Mental Illness*. London: Paladin.

Tang, K.L. and Cheung, C.K. (2007) 'The Competence of Social Work Students Working with Victims of the 2004 Tsunami Disaster', *International Social Work*, 50(3): 405–18.

Tapley, J. (2002) Victims' Rights: A Critical Examination of the British Criminal Justice System from the Victims' Perspectives. Unpublished Ph. D. thesis. Southampton University, Social Work Studies.

Training Organization for the Personal Social Services (TOPSS) (2002) *The National Occupational Standards for Social Work*. London: TOPSS.

Turning Point (2004) *People Not Problems*. London: Turning Point.

Utting, W. (1991) *Children in Public Care*. London: HMSO.

Wagner, G. (1988) *Residential Care: A Positive Choice*. London: HMSO.

Walton, R. (1975) *Women in Social Work*. London: Routledge and Kegan Paul.

Warner, N. (1992) *Choosing to Care*. London: HMSO.

Warren, J. (2007) *Service User and Carer Participation in Social Work*. Exeter: Learning Matters.

Waterhouse, R. (2000) *Lost in Care: Report on Child Abuse in North Wales*. London: The Stationery Office.

Watt, N. (2007) 'Rethink over Immigrants', *The Observer*, 20 May.

Wendell, S. (1996) *The Rejected Body: Feminist Philosophical Reflections on Disability*. London: Routledge.

Wild, J. (ed.) (1999) *Working with Men For Change*. London: UCL Press.

Wolfenberger, W. (1972) *The Principle of Normalisation in the Human Services*. Toronto: National Institute on Mental Retardation.

Woodcock, J. (2003) 'The Social Work Assessment of Parenting: An Exploration', *British Journal of Social Work*, 33(1): 87–106.

Woodward, W. (2008) 'Government Drive to Ensure that "Every Older Person Matters"', *The Guardian*, 5 January.

Young, J. (1999) *The Exclusive Society: Social Exclusion, Crime and Difference in Late Modernity*. London: Sage.

Younghusband, E. (1964) *Social Work with Families: Readings in Social Work*. London: Allen and Unwin.

Younghusband, E. (1978) *Social Work in Britain, 1950–1975*. London: Allen and Unwin.

Author Index

Subject Index